1996

1-800-PRESIDENT

THE REPORT *of the* TWENTIETH CENTURY FUND TASK FORCE ON TELEVISION AND THE CAMPAIGN OF 1992

1-800-PRESIDENT

With Background Papers by

Kathleen Hall Jamieson ■ Ken Auletta ■ Thomas E. Patterson

1993 ● The Twentieth Century Fund Press ● New York

Library of Congress Cataloging-in-Publication Data

Twentieth Century Fund, Task Force on Television and the Campaign of 1992
      1-800-PRESIDENT: The Report of the Twentieth Century Fund Task Force on Television and the Campaign of 1992/ with background papers by Kathleen Hall Jamieson, Ken Auletta, Thomas E. Patterson.
      p.   cm.
      Includes Index.
      ISBN 0-87078-349-1: $9.95
      1. Television in politics--United States. 2. Presidents--United States--Election. 3. Mass media--political aspects. I. Jamieson, Kathleen Hall. II. Auletta, Ken III. Patterson, Thomas E.
      IV. Title.
      HE8700.76.U6T94 1993
      324.7'3'0973--dc20

          93-9722
          CIP

FOREWORD

The election of 1992 preserved Ronald Reagan's record as the only president since Eisenhower to complete two full terms. Chance, of course, has played a major role in this quirk of modern American history, but so has the unhappiness of voters. Their frustration with Vietnam and Watergate has evolved into a seemingly chronic bad temper about the nation's political leadership. In 1992, for example, measures to limit the terms of state and federal legislators were approved in all fourteen states in which they appeared on the ballot.

Among the numerous polls and surveys that reveal the extent to which Americans have lost faith in their leaders, two statistics from a 1992 survey stand out: 80 percent of Americans in that poll said they believed that government favors the rich and powerful, up from 29 percent in 1964, and 65 percent said they believed that "quite a few" government officials are corrupt (in 1976, even in the wake of Watergate, only 45 percent believed that to be the case). This widespread discontent may be no more than the typical turmoil and background noise of our polyglot democratic system, temporarily exacerbated by economic hard times and governmental gridlock. There is evidence, however, that the sources of the public's anger are more deeply rooted.

The negative, divisive nature of recent political campaigns and the harsh portrayal of politics and politicians in the press, combined with the ongoing economic crunch facing America's families, has sharply reduced the public's respect for those in political life. Some would argue, of course, that virtually all the damage is self-inflicted: if the public believes politicians to be corrupt, perhaps it is because of all the scandals in which politicians have been involved. Moreover, political coverage is bound to have a sharper edge when it reflects one of the obvious social trends of our era: the seeming abandonment of the notion of privacy.

v

The growth of mass media, especially television, also has increased the impact of character questions, adding seemingly to the public's negative attitude toward politics. In today's political discourse, whenever the so-called character issue is raised, however flimsy the basis, it seizes center stage, often to the exclusion of other news about campaigns and government. While character questions usually are first raised by rival politicians or the tabloids, the mainstream press has been a willing accomplice. There are numerous possible explanations, many of substance, for the carnival atmosphere and sensational news focus. One obvious one is that this stuff sells. In this sense, the coverage of campaigns may well be getting closer to a pure market outcome for the news *business*, which may not be surprising given how rapidly the "media" are changing in terms of ownership, technology, purpose, and format. (Perhaps the really amazing thing is that there was so *much* restraint in past political coverage.)

None of this, however, has made the press very popular; indeed, public hostility toward the media matches and may even exceed the bad feelings about officeholders. As the press has loomed ever larger in the electoral process (partly because parties, leaders, and other intermediaries have been swept away), it may well be assuming, at least in the public's mind, an ever larger share of responsibility for election outcomes. But most thoughtful journalists describe their growing influence as something that they neither have sought nor find particularly desirable. They recognize the importance of their role in the campaign process, but do not want to become by default the major definers of issues and candidates.

◆   ◆   ◆

Negative politics, attack advertising, and rough press coverage seemed to reach a new level of pervasiveness during the 1988 presidential campaign. Then in early 1992, Americans found themselves in the midst of an unsettling presidential campaign. Television coverage was intense, yet no one seemed happy with it. The early media coverage of the campaign justifiably provoked reactions that varied from disappointment to nothing short of outrage. The emphasis on gossip, scandal, trivia—what's called "tabloid journalism"—was decried by citizens, politicians, scholars, and media representatives themselves. Indeed, during the first quarter of the election year, the only issue on which the campaigners and the public all agreed was that television seemed less concerned with the profound issues at stake in the election than with matters of peripheral, personal, and even prurient interest.

In this context, the Twentieth Century Fund, like other organizations in and outside the press and politics, felt an obligation to examine the causes of this apparent deterioration of public discourse. In the past, we sponsored a series of projects designed to explore the implications for American democracy of this seeming devolution of the electoral process. Our reports have examined such diverse issues as the effects of television on presidential elections (*Presidential Television* by Newton Minow, Lee Mitchell, and John Bartlow Martin), the problems of coverage of international events (*International News Services* by Jonathan Fenby), the relationship between government and the press (*Press Freedoms under Pressure: The Report of the Task Force on the Government and the Press* and *A Free and Responsive Press: The Report of the Task Force for a National News Council*), and the issue of televised presidential debates (*With the Nation Watching: Report of the Twentieth Century Fund Task Force on Televised Presidential Debates, Beyond Debate, For Great Debates*, and *A Proper Institution*). The Fund is currently supporting a number of projects in this area: a series of papers on Perspectives on the News, including *The New News v. The Old News*, two essays devoted to an examination of the press and politics in the 1990s; a task force examining the future of public television; an exploration of the issues involved in the transition to a global information economy; a paper series examining the issues surrounding the concentration of media ownership, jointly sponsored with the Joan Shorenstein Barone Center at Harvard University; and a book-length examination of politics in the telecommunications age.

Although the group assembled to discuss television coverage of the 1992 presidential campaign resembled traditional Fund task forces, it placed considerably less emphasis on reaching consensus about specific policy recommendations, the normal product of such a venture. There are, of course, a host of causes for the state of nation's political culture at any given time. The focus on television in the pages that follow by no means is meant to suggest that it or even the press in general deserves the lion's share of the blame for the state of elections in the United States. For decades television, nevertheless, has been blamed for the decay in the American political process. Reforms have been proposed by the carload to little or no avail. When so much effort produces so little effect, it seems certain that something might be wrong with the criticism as well as the criticized.

Those gathered together to discuss these issues included senior, experienced, and influential individuals from the press, politics, and academia willing to take a fresh look at television coverage of the unfolding campaign. The discussions were framed and informed by presentations on the history of media campaign coverage by Kathleen Hall Jamieson, dean of the Annenberg School; reports by Marvin Kalb and Ellen Hume on the Barone Center's monitoring of network and local coverage of the 1992 campaign; and the analyses by the Freedom Forum, led by Ev Dennis, of how television news organizations deployed their resources during the campaign. In addition, the papers that are included in this volume (prepared by three distinguished observers of politics: Kathleen Hall Jamieson, Ken Auletta, and Thomas Patterson) provided valuable background information.

If nothing else, the Task Force provided a lively setting in which some of the most prominent men and women in the media and politics informally and candidly discussed the wealth of information and ideas already in the public domain—as well as new data and opinions generated in the heat of the campaign. From the Fund's point of view, if these exchanges prompt effective recommendations on the role of television in our political campaigns, we will be enormously gratified, but if not, we will be more than satisfied with the participants' enriched understanding of the media and our political process.

◆   ◆   ◆

This Report includes, in addition to three papers, a summary of the group's conversations and conclusions. These reflections recognize that campaigns and their coverage are part of the ongoing process of American democracy. In this sense, there can be no statement of final conclusions, no list of definitive remedies. What there must be, however, and what this group engaged in, is continuing debate, self-criticism, and reform of the way in which we choose our national leaders. In fact, one outcome of the discussions was a decision by the Fund that, over the next year or so, we will again look at the issue of presidential campaign debates.

In addition to thanking all those who participated, on behalf of the Fund's trustees, I want to express our special appreciation to Ben Bradlee for chairing the sessions; to Ellen Chesler, a Fund fellow who served as executive director of the group; to Michelle Miller, our vice president for program; to Will Wechsler, an intern who made immense contributions to this project; and to the three authors of the background papers. I also especially want to thank the senior anchors, producers, and executives of the networks for their willingness to participate in these deliberations. Their commitment of time and candor shows how seriously they take their responsibilities.

◆   ◆   ◆

A free society ultimately is very dependent on its press. And while technology and cultural changes have dramatically altered the nature of journalism, our dependence upon it, if anything, has grown even greater. Perhaps no one would have designed a system in which democratic education and practice was so subject to media continually pressured by financial considerations. But the marketplace also frees our media from reliance on party or government for support—no trivial virtue. On the whole, in fact, the Great Republic coexists quite nicely with selfishness, greed, and the drive for votes on the one hand and market share on the other.

And while we understand that, to be truly free, a press must be unencumbered by public rules and regulations, we surely do not mean that an unexamined press is worth having. Moreover, the very professionalism so treasured by members of the fourth estate must stand for more than simply what sells. At a minimum, we can hope for an increase in peer pressure among journalists: more shame and guilt for the bad actors and, alternatively, more approval and applause for those who cover campaigns responsibly.

Democracy thrives in an atmosphere of open debate and criticism. By coming to grips with the issues raised by recent campaign coverage, the representatives of the media and the others on our Task Force surely have shown themselves to be motivated by values that stretch well beyond monetary reward. While there is plenty of room for improvement in the press and in politics, it was impossible to come away from these deliberations without coming to one very simple but reassuring conclusion: integrity, self-criticism, and perhaps most importantly, good citizenship are alive and well at the highest levels of American journalism.

Richard C. Leone, *President*
The Twentieth Century Fund
April 1993

CONTENTS

Members of the Task Force

Benjamin C. Bradlee, *Chairman*
Vice President at Large
The Washington Post

David Aaron
Senior Fellow, The Twentieth Century Fund

R. W. Apple, Jr.
Washington Bureau Chief, *The New York Times*

Ken Auletta
Media Columnist, *The New Yorker,* and author of *Three Blind Mice:
How the TV Networks Lost Their Way*

Douglas L. Bailey
Founder and Chairman, American Political Network

Tom Brokaw
Anchor and Managing Editor, "NBC Nightly News with Tom Brokaw"

Lester M. Crystal
Executive Producer, "The MacNeil/Lehrer NewsHour"

Robert Curvin
Director, Urban Poverty Program, Ford Foundation

Everette E. Dennis
Executive Director, The Freedom Forum Media Studies Center at
Columbia University

Peter M. Flanigan
Director, Dillon, Read & Co., Inc.

Paul Friedman
Executive Vice President, ABC News

Suzanne Garment
Resident Scholar, American Enterprise Institute for Public Policy
Research

Ellen Hume
Senior Fellow and Adjunct Lecturer, Joan Shorenstein Barone Center
on the Press, Politics and Public Policy, John F. Kennedy School of
Government at Harvard University

Kathleen Hall Jamieson
Dean and Professor of Communication, The Annenberg School for
Communication at the University of Pennsylvania

Peter Jennings
Anchor and Senior Editor, "World News Tonight with Peter
Jennings,"ABC News

Marvin Kalb
Director, Joan Shorenstein Barone Center on the Press, Politics and
Public Policy, John F. Kennedy School of Government at Harvard
University

James A. Leach
Representative, First Congressional District, Iowa

Nancy Weiss Malkiel
Dean of the College and Professor of History, Princeton University

Thomas E. Patterson
Professor, The Maxwell School of Citizenship and Public Affairs,
Syracuse University

Nelson W. Polsby
Director of the Institute of Governmental Studies and Professor of
Political Science at the University of California, Berkeley

David H. Sawyer
Chairman, Sawyer/Miller Group

Adele Smith Simmons
President, John D. and Catherine T. MacArthur Foundation

Theodore C. Sorensen
Senior Partner, Paul, Weiss, Rifkind, Wharton & Garrison

John F. Stacks
Deputy Managing Editor, *Time* magazine

Ed Turner
Executive Vice President, CNN

Lane Venardos
Vice President for Hard News and Special Events, CBS News

Ellen Chesler
Fellow, The Twentieth Century Fund, ***Task Force Executive Director***

REPORT OF THE TASK FORCE

Early in 1992, the Twentieth Century Fund decided to gather a group of thoughtful and influential individuals from the press, politics, academia, and the financial and the foundation communities to examine television's influence on the year's unfolding presidential election. Commercial television has long been a favorite target of those who decry its powerful—and, some say, perverse—influence on American politics. And the need for systematic, timely, and thoughtful appraisals of the coverage of national political campaigns is universally acknowledged.

More than twenty-five years ago, the Fund first recommended that Congress demand free time on television for presidential candidates, that uniform standards for presidential debates be adopted, and that other reforms be made. The 1992 Task Force on Television and the Campaign of 1992 was thus quite consciously convened to bring together diverse opinions in a reconsideration of old and perhaps intractable problems.

A fresh look seemed particularly warranted in light of developments since 1988, a year in which virtually no one escaped criticism for the especially base level of the nation's political discourse. The general malaise over politics that year had prompted considerable investments of both money and effort in empirical research and theoretical scholarship, much of which produced practical proposals for reform.

A few of these, including suggestions for analyzing the content of advertising and for expanding the length of sound bites, were adopted by the television industry and seemed worthy of tracking. At the same time, many more proposals—such as a recommendation for dedicated coverage of issues and candidates on the nine Sundays preceding the election—simply languished, leaving questions about whether something might be wrong with the criticism as well as the criticized.

The 1992 Task Force met three times in the summer and fall. Three papers by experts in the field of media studies were commissioned to stimulate discussion. The first paper, by Kathleen Hall Jamieson, dean of the Annenberg School for Communication at the University of Pennsylvania, provided essential background by summarizing a wide range of specific technical aspects of conventional television reporting that have been analyzed in recent years, calling particular attention to the tendency of reporters to focus on campaign strategy at the expense of substantive issues. The second paper, by Ken Auletta, author and the *New Yorker*'s media columnist, looked directly at the primary campaigns of 1992 and examined the changing role of traditional reporting by the "boys (and girls) on the bus." Auletta argues that the often insectlike behavior of the press drives candidates to seek unfiltered means of communicating with voters. And the third paper, by Professor Thomas Patterson of Syracuse University, took a longer view by asking whether the tension and drama that drive good television journalism, whatever its format, can ever be fully reconciled with the needs and best interests of a democratic political system that must build consensus and promote common values. Patterson calls for a reevaluation of "objectivity" and a reconsideration of the traditionally adversarial relationship between politicians and the press.

Their papers are reprinted here, along with an edited transcript of the often spirited discussion that followed each formal presentation. Speakers are not only edited in the Synopses of the Meetings but also quoted anonymously, not so much to protect the innocent as to permit the reader to concentrate on the content without becoming distracted by personality. Preliminary research from the Joan Shorenstein Barone Center and a series of reports from the Freedom Forum Media Studies Center at Columbia University were presented to our Task Force in the hope of bringing the broadest possible perspective to the group, and some of those findings are also covered in the Synopses.

None of our participants could have anticipated the dramatic changes that took place in 1992 in the presidential campaign itself and in television coverage. Two factors were at work: A laggard economy dramatically reawakened voter interest in politics, and several savvy, insurgent candidates exploited the new technologies that for the first time allowed direct access via television to potential supporters. Watching these historic developments as they progressed made the work of the Task Force especially compelling.

While there were substantial differences of opinion and disagreements among Task Force participants—especially between practicing journalists and scholars—exchanges were always considerate, and the Task Force was able to identify several prevailing concerns and to reach a few tentative conclusions about how television covers the presidential campaign.

IMPROVEMENTS IN 1992

The Task Force acknowledges the improvements made in 1992, particularly by the nightly network news programs, which instituted reforms that limited the influence of political handlers and that gave more attention to substantive campaign issues. Working journalists and academics alike generally agreed that the following developments made 1992 a better year for television news.

LESS RELIANCE ON PHOTO OPPORTUNITIES

The most visible and effective reform was the general refusal to allow staged photo opportunities to direct national news coverage. Whereas visuals from "Morning in America" dominated the networks in 1984, and visits to flag factories and recitations of the pledge of allegiance manipulated the coverage in 1988, there were fewer photo ops in 1992. This development did not happen by chance: "We all learned how to get away from the photo op," as one prominent journalist explained. "Among other things, we took our best people off the buses and the airplanes." Other members of the Task Force, however, argued that the best way to avoid the negative effects of photo ops was not by taking the finest reporters off the buses but by ensuring that they provide context for their stories and exercise sound journalistic judgment when they air visuals staged by the campaigns.

LONGER SOUND BITES

The expanded reporting of candidates' stump speeches on the "MacNeil/Lehrer NewsHour" and the conscious effort by CBS to lengthen the standard campaign sound bite (though tracking showed CBS did not always succeed) were improvements that began to address demands for more informative, nuanced coverage.

INCREASED ISSUE COVERAGE

The national news shows also increased their issue coverage through expanded reporting of the lead stories of the day, and through special nightly segments analyzing issues of voter interest.

CRITIQUES OF CAMPAIGN COMMERCIALS

Additionally, the commercial networks, public television, and especially CNN aired "ad watches" exposing paid political advertisements and "infomercials" that sought to deliberately mislead the public. Considering the impact such negative commercials as "Willie Horton" had on the previous presidential election, television should be commended for treating campaign advertisements as legitimate subjects for scrutiny.

BENEFITS OF THE "NEW NEWS"

The serendipitous ascension of the "new news" in 1992—such as "Larry King Live," MTV, and local news programs—has had great significance. Combined with the information now available on continuous cable news broadcasts like CNN and C-SPAN, the rise of the "new news" greatly increased the number of encounters between candidates and voters. And much of this "new news" allowed something that traditional formats cannot: direct communication with average Americans. On the network morning shows and call-in talk shows, often with studio audiences, candidates appeared for hours at a time, their unfiltered statements broadcast nationwide to voters who could call in with questions of their own. This new format, in turn, stimulated conventional news broadcasts to present more "audience voices" by interviewing average voters about the campaign. At this point, it is not clear whether such broadcasting displaced more substantive coverage.

OLD AND NEW CONTROVERSIES

While television has been, and should be, applauded for making constructive changes in 1992, some habitual problems remain, and new ones have developed as a result of increased coverage in nontraditional settings.

DRAWBACKS OF THE "NEW NEWS"

Substandard journalistic practices, particularly on evening tabloid shows and daytime talk shows, "trickled up" on too many occasions and affected mainstream reporting. The "Gennifer" and "Jennifer" stories, for example, were each broken by the print tabloids, yet quickly found their way into traditional channels through a domino effect best described as a "feeding frenzy."

It was the consensus of our Task Force that neither of these stories met meaningful journalistic standards at the time of their release, yet most members felt that once the stories were "out there," even the most cautious journalists had no choice but to report them. In many instances—not just these two most notorious—the established media were no longer able to act as "gatekeepers" or "filters" of public information. To a great degree, that role is now unfilled. Furthermore, members of the Task Force also criticized the "new news" for not asking probing or substantive questions of the candidates. Permitting candidates to speak directly to the public is beneficial, but allowing candidates to freely lie or mislead unchallenged by questions seeking clarification is not responsible journalism.

The Task Force considered the dilemma of how to achieve reasonable standards for political coverage in formats that are not governed by traditional journalistic practices, without compromising freedom of speech. The need to involve the entertainment divisions, as well as the news divisions, of broadcast companies was recognized. Most of the Task Force members agreed that, in the end, the problem can probably only be resolved through a serious commitment by the industry to exercise good judgment. As a practical matter, this prescriptive may call on established journalistic institutions to limit the exposure they give to stories judged unnewsworthy in their own right—as, for example, the four television news networks and the *New York Times*, the *Washington Post,* and the *Wall Street Journal,* among others, did in their initial Gennifer Flowers coverage in 1992. To recommend that journalists and entertainment programmers alike practice good judgment seems self-evident but is nevertheless important in this context.

Recognizing the importance of peer pressure among reporters, the Task Force emphasized the value of continually and publicly exhorting traditional news divisions to exercise intelligent, judicious restraint in reporting matters of personal, prurient interest made public by tabloids, talk shows, and other entertainment formats. At the same time, the Task Force expressed concern that the producers of these new entertainment outlets often fail to recognize their responsibility to the public, not just to ratings, when interviewing political candidates.

Concern was voiced as well over the tendency of local news shows to save money by broadcasting satellite feeds produced by political campaigns without direct attribution, while also presenting staged local appearances by presidential candidates without a framework of reporting that calls attention to the format's packaged, partisan content. With surveys showing that more and more Americans receive most of their information about politics from network and local news broadcasts, and with television intent on trimming costs, the need to guard against a conflation of partisanship and business is ever greater.

The Task Force suggested that video news releases, video news conferences, satellite feeds, and infomercials produced directly by political campaigns be clearly attributed throughout their broadcast, and that their partisan nature be more carefully distinguished from professional news reporting.

As noted earlier, one of the positive features of the "new news" formats is the direct communication they provide between candidates and voters. This opportunity, however, should not depend on the whims of a patchwork of talk-show hosts.

In view of the high ratings received in 1992 by morning shows' candidate call-ins and Ross Perot's infomercials, the Task Force discussed the question of providing presidential candidates with large blocks of airtime. Some participants thought that existing proposals for legislatively mandated free time may be heavy-handed. The public's demonstrated interest in viewing the presidential candidates through a direct and unfiltered medium is evidence that such forums can be supported commercially. Others argued that the 1992 election was unusual in the amount of voter interest it generated, and that future campaigns might readily revert to old practices. There was consensus on the value of direct communication between candidates and voters, but also concern about the practice of selling time only to those who can afford to pay for it personally.

The Task Force agreed upon the need for television to institutionalize opportunities for unfiltered communication between presidential candidates and the electorate. Although the Task Force sharply divided over proposals for free time, it agreed that the question of who pays for the unfiltered communication—government, candidate, or broadcaster—should be revisited as part of the continued attention to political reform that Congress has promised.

PROFUSION OF NEGATIVE CAMPAIGN COVERAGE ON THE NETWORKS

In reaction to increased candidate exposure, many established journalists seemed all the more driven in 1992 to a cynicism that often resulted in their ascribing hidden motives to every action or statement by a candidate. For example, very rarely was a story aired about George Bush's support for private-school vouchers without reference to how this issue might help him with Catholic voters. As one Task Force participant put it, "This invites the electorate to assume that the candidate is not sincere and is not acting in the best interest of the country . . . [while] those who work for the candidate believe that it's possible to both be strategic and to be acting in the best interest of the country."

This disbelief surfaced most apparently in the "kickers" or "stingers" reporters place at the end of campaign stories, which are often little more than sneers, implicitly impugning someone's—most often the candidate's—integrity. "This is the greatest complaint I hear from both sides of the aisle, and this tendency seems to be growing, not diminishing, over time," one Task Force participant commented. "I think part of the reason behind it is that it's how some people make names for themselves in the business." Another summed up a palpable sense within the group: "It's the sneer, the smirk, the choice of language, and the often snap and harsh judgments that are made on the fly that bother people."

The Task Force considered whether these closing statements confuse editorializing with what has traditionally been thought of as more "objective" reporting, and thereby reinforce public cynicism about the credibility of not only politicians but of journalists as well. Worried about this tendency, one representative from the networks noted: "It's part of the presentation we give to new people that come to our staff in Washington. We tell them to please be skeptical, but please don't be cynical. Because if you're cynical, you're brain-dead."

Recognizing the difference between thoughtful analysis and cynical attempts to sabotage a candidate's message, the Task Force agreed that television news editors, producers, and reporters themselves should seek to end or drastically reduce the practice of closing conventional campaign reports with editorial "kickers" or "stingers."

Beyond voluntary compliance, it may be worthwhile to institute some evaluation tools so that consciousness is raised about these practices and their effects, much as "ad watches" have reduced one corrosive influence of campaign handlers. Although there is some truth to the maxim that no institution is more sensitive to bad press than the press, self-criticism is a critical component of responsible journalism.

The Task Force commended the efforts of some television news organizations to sponsor an "ombudsman" or some alternative form of an electronic "letters to the editor" arrangement that allows for public commentary and critique of their professional practices.

Peer pressure and peer recognition can be extremely powerful motivational tools for journalists, but television reporters are rarely held accountable—or rewarded—for their efforts. (A visible exception in 1992 was the *New Republic*'s weekly "Clinton Suck-Up Watch," which received widespread attention and became a kind of "Hall of Shame," even though it sometimes slipped into cynicism by confusing merited praise with idolatry.) Publicly rewarding reporters, much as publicly embarrassing them, may go a long way toward promoting improved political reporting. But individual recognition from awards given in television news, such as the Alfred I. du Pont-Columbia University Awards, the Peabody Awards, and the Emmys, is often not as esteemed as that from the Pulitzer and other print prizes. What is more, existing prizes modeled on the print awards often seem only to reward reporters who uncover corruption or scandal.

As one member of the Task Force explained, "We see a lack of a serious effort by journalists to cover risk-taking politics and problem-solving. That effort does not come close to the effort reporters make in covering negative news like scandals and corruption. . . . The Pulitzer Prizes go for the scandals; they don't go for publicly identifying the risk-takers, the people with political courage."

The Task Force suggested that a study be made of existing prizes for television news coverage, with special attention to how they are administered and awarded. Foundations and other institutions should be encouraged to support awards that are as prestigious, financially rewarding, and highly visible as the best prizes for print journalism. Specific rewards should also be developed for reporting that is educational and analytic, not just searching for scandal.

TV Coverage of the Economy

If, as most observers feel, the 1992 election ultimately rested on the public's perception of the national economy, then, as one Task Force member said, "it was probably more important how we covered the economy during the campaign than anything we said about the campaign." Yet the record of televised economic coverage is disturbing. "We screwed it up," another participant stated frankly. "You know," said another, "some economic news actually is good news, but the story is always 'Economic indicators are up, but . . .'"

Why is this so? It was generally agreed that few reporters are well informed about economics. "We don't understand economics," one professional bluntly explained. Another elaborated: "There is a historic tendency in journalism to separate political and economic reporters. . . . Economic reporters never become anything else, yet you can be a specialist in the atomic bomb and end up anywhere." And a television news executive added, "There is still something worrisome about how every time an economic statistic comes out, we report it but then have to say, 'On the other hand. . . .'" Television news tends to search for a single story line or narrative, lacking the time and often the expertise to explore a complicated subject.

The Task Force expressed concern about the condition of televised reporting on the national economy, particularly the way economic issues are discussed in the context of a presidential campaign. Improvements would require news programs to rely less on political reporters for covering economic news, and instead to invest in new and creative formats for economic coverage. At the same time, the Task Force believes that media scholars should concentrate more of their studies on the manner in which economic issues are presented on television.

Beyond improvements in economic reporting, midcareer educational programs through sabbaticals or summer forums that immerse reporters in substantive policy analysis and in an evaluation of the ethical and political implications of their reporting, along the lines suggested by Task Force observer Jay Rosen, ought to be supported as well. Yale Law School's sabbatical program for journalists is a worthy example. In recognition of their enhanced stature as reporters of national stories, local news correspondents should be especially encouraged to take part in these educational opportunities. Bringing more working journalists into contact with media centers at the major universities may, in turn, improve the quality and practical orientation of media scholarship.

The Task Force encouraged foundations and academic institutions to join together to sponsor more midcareer educational programs through sabbaticals or summer forums that immerse reporters in economics and other substantive policy issues and in analysis of the ethical and political implications of their reporting.

FAILURE OF OTHER INSTITUTIONS

Many of the charges commonly leveled at the media (and at television in particular) may be misdirected. Television alone cannot transform campaigns into intelligent and profound public discourse when presidential candidates routinely seek to avoid issues, when they dwell on the opposition's negatives, and when they consciously distort.

In years past, many institutions—families, churches, community organizations, schools, and especially local political parties and their apparatus—helped to foster political awareness and to transmit values. But the authority of many of these institutions has waned, leaving television with undue influence and a role in fostering consensus that it was never designed to play.

As one journalist on the Task Force explained, "The interests and instincts of journalism can go counter to the interests and instincts of what you have to do to govern. . . . It can be a fundamental conflict . . . involving our preoccupation with covering conflict and headlines and process instead of governance." Another agreed: "Television news coverage has become a much larger part of our political system than it was thirty years ago, in the absence of other competing institutions that might send different types of messages." A third also ardently agreed, arguing that "the press doesn't have the incentives or the accountability or the values to provide political arrangements."

The Task Force recognized the need to enhance the educational opportunities available to voters through local schools, civic organizations, churches, political parties, and other voluntary institutions that we rely on to help transmit positive political values and build responsible citizenship. Just as we strive to foster the development of democratic institutions in Russia and Eastern Europe, foundations and other institutions in America should seek to develop an array of public-private partnerships to do so here at home.

Addendum

by Everette Dennis

I think it is fair to say that some of us on the Task Force think the "sound bite" business is a canard. If identifying this as an issue helps us to take a stand against shallow reporting, that is fine, but, in and of itself, the length of a sound bite is actually peripheral to the larger question of whether something is covered thoroughly and well. Print stories are pieced together from lengthy interviews and other material which are often adequately reduced to a single line or even a phrase. These print "sound bites" are even shorter than the ones on television, and they do no harm in a balanced, thoroughly researched, professional piece of journalism.

Another point that was overlooked by the Task Force was that television did quite a good job this time with critical fact-checking, especially after the debates. For example, if a candidate made a specific claim backed by statistics that were patently wrong or used out of context, television reporters and commentators said so. That is a great improvement.

One final note: Maybe the best thing that came out of this Task Force was the process itself. To an outsider, the fact that top people from the media, academia, and politics actually talked to each other during the campaign might not seem like much, but to those of us who study the media and politics, providing an opportunity for these people to converse in a nondefensive fashion, while keeping the public interest squarely in mind, was recognized as quite an accomplishment.

ADDENDUM

BY ELLEN HUME

A sking that news organizations use "intelligent, judicious restraint" is noble, but I think we can be more helpful than that, without treading on the First Amendment.

I would suggest, in particular, that news organizations broaden the definition of "character" to put such matters as sex scandals in context. Perhaps what we need to do is to look at "public" character the way Missouri state representative Karen McCarthy, president-elect of the National Conference of State Legislatures, suggests we evaluate each and every candidate for public office. This would require the media to ask:

▲ Is your word good, or do you talk one way and act another?

▲ Does what you do in private life affect your public performance?

▲ Do you stand up for your beliefs and go against the public tide or the special interests when you think it is needed for the public good?

▲ What is your value system?

▲ Do you use good or bad judgment?

▲ Are you willing to use your political capital to accomplish something you think is necessary?

To this list I would add another question: Do you use your public power for the private gain of yourself, your friends, or your family?

If journalists would pursue these questions with the same vehemence they pursue issues of private sexuality, we would all have a relevant yardstick for evaluating our political leaders. After all, we're not marrying these candidates—we're trying to figure out whether or not they can govern well.

In sum, what is public character versus private character? If news organizations make a good-faith effort to examine more than just the scandal of the moment, journalists can have it both ways—keep the scandal and elevate the dialogue at the same time. In addition, the more relevant "character" qualities we examine will help the public to evaluate its leaders more effectively.

ADDENDUM

BY MARVIN KALB

A review of the draft conclusions of the Task Force on Television and the Campaign of 1992 compels me to return to the "Nine Sundays" proposal first advanced by the Joan Shorenstein Barone Center on the Press, Politics and Public Policy in September 1991. There is no doubt in my mind that television coverage of the 1992 campaign was better than anyone had expected. Roger Ailes, the GOP consultant, warned after the 1988 campaign: "If you didn't like '88, you're going to hate '92." If Ailes had been right, we'd have had every reason to "hate" the '92 campaign; but he was wrong. And he was wrong because the networks demonstrated that they were perfectly capable, in most cases, of exercising sensible and professional judgment about what's news and what isn't news, what's worthy of coverage and what isn't, what should run 9.6 seconds and what should run longer, what's truth and what's falsehood. Moreover, the networks performed these admirable editorial tasks in an environment of acute financial constraints.

The new and in some cases chronic problems that emerged in '92 demand a broader approach before they can be resolved, if indeed they can ever be. For example, the Task Force bows much too quickly to the establishment network view that if a story is "out there," it must be covered. On a Friday in January 1992, the day after the Gennifer Flowers story was faxed to news organizations by the *Star*, a supermarket tabloid, NPR's Linda Wertheimer met with her staff of "All Things Considered." How were they going to handle the story? One producer argued that the story had to be aired. Why? asked Wertheimer. Because, the producer responded, it's "out there." Fine, but that doesn't mean, Wertheimer snapped, that it has to be "in here." All stories are the result of editorial decisions— they don't happen on their own—and tougher standards are required. Even the best journalists find themselves, on occasion, swept along by the tide of competitive pressures cloaked as journalistic toughness.

Let us not forget that on the day the *Star* faxed the Flowers story to dozens of news organizations, "Nightline" went with it. At first the show thought it might have an interview with Governor Clinton, but after plans for the interview collapsed, "Nightline" still decided to go with the story, even though it had no independent corroboration. The coverage on "Nightline" provided all the legitimacy that local news needed the next day. As more local television ran with the Flowers story, more talk radio went with it too. By the following Monday, when Flowers appeared at a news conference, the story itself had reached a "critical mass," or so the journalistic rationalization went, and CNN decided to provide "live" coverage. The other networks followed in CNN's wake. The story was, after all, "out there."

Months before, NBC News had decided to use the name of an alleged rape victim in the William Kennedy Smith trial in Florida. Why? Because, it explained, the name had been used in a tabloid. Then the next morning, the *New York Times* used the name, saying that NBC had used it the evening before.

There is a gradual but indisputable blurring of the line between news and entertainment, between Ted Koppel and David Letterman, between hard and soft news, between journalists who never worked for the government and those who did; and if the American people are increasingly skeptical about the purity and reliability of news coverage they have every reason to be. That's why the candidates in '92 evaded the traditional press corps and went on the talk shows, and that's why, in this emerging age of electronic democracy, President Clinton continues to slip around the White House press corps, whenever possible, to find alternative means of talking directly to the American people. And, most disturbing, the American people seem not in the least bit upset by this phenomenon. What then becomes the future of network news? More broadly, what then becomes the shape of representative democracy?

If there is a single overarching criticism of the Task Force's report, it is that it focused too much on the trees and ignored the forest of economic and technological change that is far more important to the political process. It is in this spirit that I return to the essence of the "Nine Sundays" proposal, which attempts to address the underlying causes of discontent and disconnection between the people and the process. I start with Sissela Bok's observations that the American political process can be envisaged as a triangle with the people in one corner, the politicians in another, and the press in the third, and that if one of the three corners can be changed for the better, the other two will almost inevitably adjust to its new direction. Our assumption is that the '92 campaign demonstrates that the networks can improve their product on their own, without legislation, and this improvement can affect the entire political process in a positive way. Still left as problems are the corrupting effect of money and the erosion of journalistic standards.

"Nine Sundays" (or a variation thereof, such as Nine Occasions or Opportunities) proposes in essence that the networks provide free time to the major candidates for a substantive discussion of the major issues facing the nation.

The general-election campaign theoretically encompasses nine Sundays—from Labor Day, when the presidential campaign is presumed to begin in earnest, to Election Day, when it all comes to a blessed close. It is in this finite period of time, with interest increasing week after week, that the American people devote their attention to a key question: Who will be their next president?

In "Nine Sundays," the Joan Shorenstein Barone Center proposes that the three major networks (on a rotating basis), plus CNN, C-SPAN, and PBS, provide ninety minutes of evening or prime time for each of nine weeks (preferably on Sundays) for a serious discussion by the principal presidential candidates of the major issues (one issue at a time) that concern the American people. For example, taxes may be the subject one evening, Middle East policy or abortion another, education, the environment, or U.S.–Russian relations on the others.

Of these nine TV occasions between Labor Day and Election Day, three would be devoted to presidential debates, one to a vice-presidential debate, one to a concluding address by the major candidates, and the others to substantive programs including individual interviews with the candidates. The network news departments would decide on their own how to use their time.

Network news would be encouraged to offer this unusual series to commercial sponsorship (with advertising tastefully presented at the beginning and end of each broadcast, no interruptions in between) so that any financial losses to the networks would be limited. Given both their continuing importance as sources of news and their financial shakiness, the networks' needs must be taken into account.

If, as many scholars contend, television has become the principal means of political discourse in the United States, the "Nine Sundays" proposal is an excellent approach for elevating the discourse. This proposal is designed to provide a fixed amount of time for substantive discussion of the major problems. It ensures a serious-textured tone to overall news coverage of the presidential campaign. It gives voters regular, predictable access to the candidates over a sustained period of time. It sets a framework for constructive televised exposure to the issues, and it grows naturally out of the electronic democracy that is now evolving in our political discourse.

What is needed is a larger conceptual vision. The Task Force advances good ideas, but it does not leap far enough into the future. It does not seem to keep abreast of technological and economic changes that affect the very foundations of our form of representative democracy.

SYNOPSES OF THE

MEETINGS OF THE TASK FORCE

FIRST MEETING: JULY 15, 1992

K athleen Hall Jamieson began by elaborating on the points she made in her background paper. She showed clips of what she calls "newsads": aired reports that unintentionally reinforce previously held misconceptions about a candidate's actual position. She also played examples of typical pre- and post-debate coverage. Correspondents were shown to be eager to play the "expectations game" and to present the election in terms of the competing strategies of the campaigns. After analyzing these and other clips, she argued that network news often adopts language and visuals that originate from campaign consultants and are driven by the most recent polls. In one particular case, Jamieson noted that the visuals in a 1988 report on the candidates' positions on crime showed black criminals and white crime victims, an image that reinforced one of the strategies of the Bush campaign that played upon existing racial tensions.

Marvin Kalb and Everette Dennis followed with brief progress reports on the work being done at their institutions. In its ongoing content analysis of the nightly news coverage of the presidential campaign, the Joan Shorenstein Barone Center has found that coverage of campaign events—essentially the staged photo ops—steadily declined during the first months of coverage. Kalb also noted that while the average length of the network news sound bite hovers around nine seconds, the average increases to more than twenty seconds overall when "MacNeil/Lehrer" and "CNN Prime News" are included in the analysis. Dennis presented us with Freedom Forum's newly published report on the coverage of the presidential primaries. Its most significant finding concerns the extent to which local stations use video news releases from the campaigns in their coverage.

The discussion began when a few questions were thrown on the table. Is there any evidence that American voters want more information? Would ten-point plans by each of the candidates attract any audience at all? How many people really get their information from the "old media" anyway? Aren't they really learning about the candidates from the "new media"?

Through the ensuing conversation, Task Force members reached a consensus on some of these important concerns. They agreed that any realistic definition of the news media must now be expanded to include many of the "new news" institutions. More than most others, this political season has made clear that the icons of the "old news"—Peter, Tom, and Dan; the *Times* and the *Post*—no longer steer political reporting. Instead, to varying degrees, they have ceded their judgment, timing, and technology to the "new news." As one person pointedly observed, the mainstream press can no longer be accused of being "gatekeepers" to public political information.

A majority of the members also agreed that the emergence of the "new" and instant news has made it extremely difficult for "old news" institutions to uphold their standards. One member noted that "people can't differentiate between 'Hard Copy' and the network news because they're all played back to back. The distinction of the station break is blurred; it's all just one news program." One reason for this phenomenon has been the network convention of giving "exclusive" footage to local affiliates, and the affiliate practice of playing that footage before the national network newscast. What would happen if the networks suddenly cut off the locals? "We would produce six hundred new clients for CNN," said one participant. Several times it was stressed that affiliates do not have news executives; they have sales executives.

The Task Force also discussed polls, their impact on campaign coverage, and their evolution over the last decades from an imprecise tool to an "exact" science. While many in the group agreed that "horserace" questions were inherently interesting, a fragile consensus emerged around some of the points Jamieson made in her presentation. Particularly, some in the group agreed that the outcomes of polls all too often shape the language and the visuals in the news reports. The symbolic moments correspondents choose to include in their reports are very different for front-runners than they are for those who are lagging in the polls. "I think we have been guilty of doing exactly that," one member said. "There's a larger point of how polls influence what stories you decide to cover and your overall view of how the campaign is going. I think our use of the polls as a crutch is insidious."

The mainstream media have been forced to cover unsubstantiated rumors that have had a significant impact on this year's presidential campaign. This, of course, was a major topic of conversation, and opinions varied among the participants. Members disagreed, for example, about whether or not the *New York Times* (and a few other members of the media) looked silly by trying to contain the Gennifer Flowers story. In fact, a good number of the members felt that the networks had no choice but to lead with the Flowers story. "We had our hands tied by the march of events," was a common sentiment. The driving force of impending deadlines was also cited as a cause for the lack of independent research into the allegations. Many people expressed their belief that in attempting to take viewers or readers into their confidence, news programs and newspapers can only look "unbelievably pompous." An opinion expressed repeatedly was that a public who has already heard about a titillating story involving a presidential candidate will only ridicule the mainstream press if it attempts to ignore the story.

So is it possible to uphold standards in this age of instant news? "There's a real answer to that," said one of the members. "Those of us who are not in the business think that you can." Another person (this one in the business) recalled when the stock market fell forty points on a rumor about George Bush's affairs, "The press was confronted with having to report a real event in the world. But we did so without explaining exactly what the rumor was." The result, he noted, was not an outraged public but, as it turned out, a story that faded away in a day. "This was an example of standards being applied." Could this type of reporting be applied to presidential campaigns? More generally, is it likely that such standards could be applied consistently? The question was left unanswered.

SECOND MEETING: OCTOBER 23, 1992

Everette Dennis opened the meeting with a summary of the Freedom Forum's latest report, "An Uncertain Season: Reporting in the Postprimary Period."Focusing on the importance of the "new news" in this year's campaign coverage, the report confirms the conventional wisdom that radio and television talk shows had emerged as a staple of this year's campaign, achieving "enormous influence." Yet the report shows that this new influence was not uniformly anticipated or understood by the presidential candidates: Bill Clinton made nineteen appearances on the network morning talk shows from January to June, and Ross Perot made ten, but George Bush seemed notably reluctant to enter the talk-show circuit, appearing only twice.

Dennis also reported that, for the first time, three talk-show hosts (Larry King, Arsenio Hall, and Phil Donahue) moved into the ranks of the top-ten "pundits" most frequently mentioned in a statistical search of articles and programs from leading press outlets. But what kinds of questions did candidates face from these hosts? Just how did they compare with those asked by journalists? Freedom Forum's research suggests that "talk show listeners and viewers frequently pose concise, issue-driven queries to presidential candidates during talk show appearances" [from the report].

Dennis also described another phenomenon that emerged in 1992: the numerous methods by which candidates bypassed the mainstream media and communicated directly with voters. Among these were toll-free and fee-based phone numbers, on-line computer services, video cassettes, and the transmission of video via satellite. In all, media-watchers were struck by "a great sense of movement regarding who was covering what, and a reliance on unusual and entertainment-oriented sources."

Ellen Hume then summarized some of the ongoing research of the Joan Shorenstein Barone Center, highlighting data that show the difference in tone among the networks' campaign coverage before the conventions, from February 1 to June 4. These findings show that ABC consistently presented the candidates more positively than did either NBC or CBS; NBC was the most neutral of the three networks, particularly in their visual material. Hume also reported that all the broadcast networks were more critical of President Bush than of any of the other five candidates during this period. She quoted the center's report: "Whether because of his association with the bad economic news, the criticism of opponents in both parties, or the adversarial approach of the White House press corps, President Bush obtained relatively low marks from the news on ABC, CBS, or NBC." By contrast, Ross Perot received significantly favorable coverage from television news.

Researchers at the Joan Shorenstein Barone Center also addressed political advertising, finding that President Bush's ads were more negative and less effective than those of the other major candidates during the primary season. Fifty-nine percent of Bush's ads were judged to be either negative or leaning negative. This was followed by Jerry Brown (50 percent negative), Paul Tsongas (39 percent negative), Pat Buchanan (16 percent negative), and Bill Clinton (14 percent negative). While continuing to be dissatisfied with the news media's coverage of the campaign in general, the public, according to Hume, has been pleased with the increased television analysis of campaign advertising.

Elaborating on his background paper, Ken Auletta followed with some reflections on this year's campaign coverage. While acknowledging many of the improvements the media made compared to coverage of the 1988 campaign, he nonetheless criticized a continued penchant for "gang-like conformity" or, as he put it, a point at which "the critical mass loses its mind." As an example, he cited the "feeding frenzies" surrounding the "Gennifer" and "Jennifer" stories. Second, he said we have witnessed how the very form of journalism itself—the search for the new and the "conflictive"—still shapes content. When a lone Act Up activist heckled Clinton in New York, and when the POW families protested in front of Bush in July, he explained, the media responded by portraying candidates as losing their cool even when they did not. "Our tendency to look for conflict was more on display than their tendency to lose their cool." Third, Auletta described how competition with entertainment programs has given the press a tendency to transform politics into soap opera. The "Murphy Brown" episode made this comparison all too apt.

Overall, Auletta divided the campaign into two periods: pre-Perot and post-Perot. Pre-Perot featured the "boys on the bus" as traditional filters of political information to the masses and operated the way the media always has. Post-Perot began with the "Larry King Show" on February 20. "It was clear then that the public was able to bypass us." So where are we now? "It seems to me," Auletta concluded, "that this campaign, when looked back upon, will be construed as a transitional campaign. The boys on the bus will have less power in the future . . . yet without potent political parties, we need an intelligent press as a filter. If we are to be that filter, we have to win back the public trust that we've lost. That is the great challenge for those of us who are proud to say we are in the media."

The discussion began with a spirited defense of television's campaign coverage, especially when compared to the coverage of four years ago, or even the coverage of seven months ago. "The turning point for me," one prominent journalist explained, "was when I woke up and realized that we were asking all these questions of Bill Clinton about Gennifer

Flowers, and all the public in New Hampshire wanted to know about was the economy." There was a particular pride in how campaign operatives have not been able to manipulate television coverage the way they did in 1984 and 1988. "You couldn't get a photo op on network television now," another explained. A third member agreed, proclaiming that "George Bush is going to have to jump naked into the Grand Canyon if he wants that backdrop."

But what about the common complaints concerning television's failure to examine substantive issues? While there was some support for this criticism (one member commented that "there are a lot of issues out there that are terribly important that have not been dealt with honestly and in great depth [by television]"), many expressed concern that television was being singled out for a problem that has many causes. Blame should be expanded properly to include the candidates ("We went up to cover a debate on the health care issue in New Hampshire . . . and these idiots couldn't speak about it"); the handlers ("When we suggested to let [the candidates] talk to each other . . . they were terrified and refused to do it"); the "new news" ("The mainstream networks only did a modest amount of coverage [of Gennifer Flowers]; most of the stuff was tabloid and local"); and the public ("They're not doing their homework"). Furthermore, one member promised, "We have six weeks of issue-oriented features prepared. I guarantee you they will get on the air every night."

Several members had more novel points to make about the press. As the news media splinters and competition becomes more fierce, one noted, individual organizations and news programs are "increasingly developing a constituency approach." Just as politicians regularly find their philosophical agenda giving way to the public's concerns, certain parts of the press (particularly much of the "new news") find themselves stretching journalistic standards to accommodate specific audiences. One example: while the mainstream press had virtually stopped reporting on Ross Perot because he was no longer as newsworthy as he once was, talk shows had not yet made that distinction. "I now think that they are cynically putting on Ross Perot again to raise their ratings," was the way another put it. Yet some took issue with this argument, especially when considering the network nightly news programs, where politics must compete with many other issues of interest to viewers. "To put it succinctly," one news executive admitted, "if that thesis were true, and if what we know about what the audience cares about is accurate, we would not be covering politics at all."

A lively debate followed Jay Rosen's idea that journalists should separate "election coverage" and "campaign coverage." "Election coverage," Rosen argued, would be about who will win in November and could be done the same way it is done currently. "Campaign coverage," however, would compel journalists to recognize that they are actors in our political system and that they should behave as such. This would require that they each determine a "desired outcome" for their actions and then act to achieve that outcome by working with other actors in the political system. This "desired outcome," in Rosen's view, would be a certain type of political discourse.

While some called this argument "excellent," "very interesting," or "terrific," many did not agree. One member said that this philosophy of journalism would represent "the kind of cooperation between journalistic elites, governmental elites, and business elites that is, in some respects, the worst kind of co-optation." Another compared its potential to the "dark ages of American journalism at the beginning of the nineteenth century," when "each newspaper started with statements of purpose and strategic plans." Others argued that journalists already determine their desired outcomes routinely. "Why do you assume that we're not thinking about that all along?" was a common sentiment. "Those decisions are made a thousand times a week all over the country by all kinds of press people." Another agreed: "We are engaged in planning, not only at our network, but at the other networks as well."

The charge was also made that the media are overly cynical about politics. "We think that it can't be that the President of the United States is simply for school vouchers," said one member, "He has to be for it because he is trying to get the Catholic vote." Another defended press cynicism as press realism: "The candidates have become so political, the handlers have become so political, that indeed, just about every speech out there is aimed at the Catholic vote or the gay vote or the Southern vote or whatever. Your people are absolutely right at reporting that." "I think the problem [of press cynicism] is even worse than that," said another, "You almost can't write a good piece about either of these candidates without winding up on the *New Republic* suck-up list." This begged the question, "Why does that stuff matter so much?" Another echoed the concern, "The cynical pose that we adopt as reporters is a common pose. . . . Why are we moved by that kind of silly peer pressure?" This question was left unanswered.

Finally, the discussion touched on some of the measures that have been proposed to reform the relationship between television and presidential campaigns. The idea debated most thoroughly was Paul Taylor's suggestion that five minutes of free time be given to each candidate on alternating nights from Labor Day to the election. "Think about this," one member said in support of Taylor's proposal, "Television is the single most powerful communication vehicle that this country has. In effect, the rules are now that from Labor Day on, except for debates and paid advertising, the candidates are not allowed to get on television to say what they want to say the way they want to say it. Everyone else is allowed to—Rush Limbaugh does, John Chancellor does. Are presidential candidates not allowed?" Others disagreed. "The public is getting an enormous amount of access to the views of these candidates," said another discussant who also took umbrage at television being singled out. "If TV, then why not papers? Why not a free full page?" Another stated flatly that free time will "never, never happen." Why? "Because they [the candidates] will pay for it, and since they'll buy it, nobody's going to give it to them for free." But should it happen anyway? "In this country I think it shouldn't," he responded, "because I've finally bought into the idea of this being a country of free enterprise."

Unfortunately, the hour was late; there was little opportunity to debate how free airtime might alter the role that campaign fund-raising plays in presidential elections, a phenomenon that was repeatedly condemned. Other possible reforms were mentioned, such as the call for a deliberative opinion poll and a recommendation that the press distinguish better between candidates' public and private characters, but these ideas were also left unexplored.

THIRD MEETING: FEBRUARY 12, 1993

T he meeting began with a presentation by Thomas Patterson based on his paper, "Let the Press Be the Press: Principles of Campaign Reform." Patterson argued that with the demise of political parties, the media has been left to organize the political system, a role it is institutionally incapable of fulfilling effectively. "The press doesn't have the incentives or the accountability or the values to provide political arrangements," he explained.

Patterson contended that this fundamental dilemma is behind many of the typical criticisms of the media, including its penchant for cynical and negative political coverage and its overwhelming interest in peripheral and prurient issues. "At root here is a difference between journalistic values, criteria, and standards and political values, criteria, and standards." This analysis was well received by several of the members. "What he is saying," one reporter elaborated, "is that the interests and instincts of journalism go counter to the interests and instincts of what you have to do to govern." Another member agreed: "The problem is that . . . television news coverage has become a much larger part of our political system than it was thirty years ago in the absence of other competing institutions that might send different messages." If this is the problem, a television news executive asked, then "what are the other institutions we should be looking at?" If the people are uninformed about their political choices, he continued, then "maybe we ought to figure out something about how we educate our children and our adults in the political process."

Patterson, by contrast, prompted a spirited debate when, instead of focusing his recommendations on institutions such as the political parties or the educational system, he examined ways that the media themselves could help solve the problem. In addition to advocating a Nine Sundays-type free airtime proposal and suggesting that the campaign be made shorter and more deliberative, Patterson recommended that members of the press refrain from "speaking for the candidates" or "judging candidates' motives." Rather than defining issues according to journalistic values (for instance, demanding that Clinton announce precisely which levels of income he would tax more), reporters should be content to report the issues as the candidates choose to define them ("Clinton says he's going to raise taxes on the wealthy").

Some politicians present agreed with this analysis. "What we have now is a huge deviation from what existed when I went to school: the understanding that the media had the primary responsibility of reporting as opposed to interpreting," one member said. "There is a sense of condescension on the part of the media, a sense that the media think people can't figure out for themselves who is and who isn't a phony. . . .

I think some folks here underestimate the ability of real people to figure out this stuff. People can figure out who's making a little bit of sense and who's not."

"I don't agree with you," a prominent reporter stated candidly. "I don't agree because we went through 'Morning in America' when the press was manipulated with pretty pictures. There was no way to penetrate." "Well, it sort of ends the discussion if you come to the conclusion that the people aren't smart enough," the politician replied. "Why can't we just give folks the opportunity to make their own determinations as opposed to filtering it for them?" Another journalist asked, "What about David Duke? Would you have us let him go? Just let them have it?" When the politician asked the journalist if he felt the public successfully saw through Duke's moderate facade, the journalist replied, "Yes. With a great deal of help from the press." "Again," the politician responded, "that sort of answers everything."

A television news executive later agreed with the politician that "people are smarter than we give them credit for." But if the public is smart enough to see through the politicians by themselves, then surely they can see through the reporters. "How can someone such as yourself who has just said that we ought to give more credit to the American people argue that people assume that [reporters] are oracles? People are smarter than that." He also noted that "you assume that there is one thing instead of a range of options available to the American people. They can watch their candidates on Larry King and then they can turn to CBS or NBC and try to find out some of the criticisms of what their candidates just said. There's a whole lot of options available to them. . . . But once you start to go down this path of saying that our job is to get out of the way, it seems that you invite more problems than you've got with the existing system, as sloppy as it is."

Another politician noted the irony in this debate between interpretation and straight reporting. "From the Republican party's perspective, the great tragedy of this election was that the press let through what the Republican party was saying. The Republican party said loud and clear, 'we are going to enter the bedroom' [and] that religion and politics mixed. No one can say that message was blocked. Likewise, Clinton said loud and clear that he was going to raise taxes on the rich and run a more aggressive, activist government. It was the Republican party that wanted to have a message and then hide it. The press [did not let them] downplay [it]. . . . In 1984 the Republican party had a very similar message, but nobody thought it was going to come to fruition. The press was so devilish by 1992 that they underscored that it might! These statements at the Convention could become reality!"

Patterson also said that reporters should bear the burden of proving that candidates are lying; unless reporters can prove otherwise, they should presume that politicians are telling the truth. In support, Patterson reiterated the point stressed in his paper that numerous studies have shown that presidential candidates have a "good record of keeping their promises." Furthermore, [from his paper] he argued that "I know of no study that supports the press's contention that candidates for the presidency regularly make promises they either cannot or will not fulfill" [from his paper]. "Unless you have really quite clear evidence for suggesting that the candidate is, in fact, trying to engage in a clear-cut deception of the electorate," Patterson said to the group, "then it doesn't serve either the electorate or the process very well to smugly suggest that truth is on your side and the only game the candidates play is deception."

This recommendation was not well received by many of the working journalists present. One reporter said public statements by politicians were "red meat" for journalists to attack, and attacked they were. Another senior journalist said bluntly that "my presumption is that any politician's public statement in a campaign is probably not true, period. . . . The powers that be in Washington have no reverence for the truth. Therefore, Tom Patterson's proposal will not be successful." This view was, in turn, assailed by several non-journalists. "[That statement] has a whole lot to do with how the press approaches everything," a politician said, "Yet I have very seldom seen a United States Government official lie." Another person remarked that "with one or two exceptions, I don't know anybody in the White House who would lie to a reporter."

To this, an incredulous journalist responded, "I know dozens, dozens that lie all the time." Another asserted that "I've been lied to so many times by your colleagues." A journalist-turned-academic agreed, saying, "I was lied to all the time as a reporter." Numerous examples were put forth as evidence that politicians often use "the big lie." When others argued these were only anecdotes which didn't prove anything, a well-known reporter noted, "Yes, Ms. Tamposi isn't all that much. And Iran-Contra isn't all that much. And Watergate isn't all that much. And Vietnam isn't all that much. And Iraqgate isn't all that much. But there is a cumulative effect."

The point was made that, perhaps, "what reporters call a lie is not what politicians call a lie." A politician present agreed: "To assume a lie is awful. . . . There is a distinction between acting self-serving and lying, and only very seldom is it crossed." Another said that most people "don't take the call or will not get into the whole issue, but they don't lie." Patterson, of course, agreed: "Your proposition that they're lying is not founded in fact. I think it's a dangerous proposition that ends up poisoning the relationship between the electorate and the candidates, and, as I argued, I think it undermines the credibility of the press."

This debate concluded as both sides seemed to compromise their extreme positions. The journalist who most adamantly held that politicians should be presumed to be lying said that "if you never repeat this, I will admit that my presumption of lying is not always right." And the politician who argued most strenuously against that view paraphrased I. F. Stone: "I believe the government tells the truth. But it's as if I was walking down a street and somebody came running out of a bank carrying a satchel full of money. And then if I was to ask him what he was doing, he'd say, 'I am waiting for a car.' He'd be telling the truth."

The Task Force then discussed the perceived negative tone of much of the campaign coverage. Some reporters denied the existence of a universally negative attitude toward politicians. "There are an awful lot of politicians who are regularly written about with great respect. When was the last time you heard anything negative about Bill Bradley? Or Dick Lugar? Or, until recently, Jim Baker?" Another disagreed, saying that "we see a lack of serious effort by journalists to cover risk-taking politics and problem solving. That effort does not come close to the effort reporters make in covering negative news, scandals, corruption, et cetera. And the Pulitzer Prizes always go for the scandals; they don't go for identifying the risk takers or the people with political courage." Still another member said that it was appropriate that the press is "cynical, skeptical, and suspicious" since the American public was as well.

Yet many academics and politicians urged the press to distinguish between "skepticism and cynicism." A few specifically singled out for criticism the "sneering" closing statements by television reporters. This complaint struck a chord in academics and some television journalists as well, who reached a consensus that the prevalence of these statements constitutes a serious problem, although some felt it was not an "epidemic" one. "This is the greatest complaint I hear from both sides of the aisle," one member reported, "that the story may be substantive, but that smirky closing twist comes in at the end." A prominent television journalist agreed: "It's the sneer, the smirk, the choice of language, the often snap and harsh judgments that are made on the fly that bother people."

Several members of the Task Force questioned the media's objectivity when they report poll results. "I can tell you that the complaint comes when the opposition has big poll results, and it's a big headline, and then when we read of good poll movements for our side it's on paragraph four," said one member who has helped manage presidential campaigns. An academic explained that this result may not be due to bias, but may instead reflect the source of the particular polls in question. "What we are finding is that newspapers were running their own polls at the top of the page but were running other people's polls at the bottom of the page," she said. A newspaperman agreed: "That we do. Totally true." Another member questioned the accuracy of typical polling results. Beyond methodological concerns, for instance, "when the public answers your questions 'Do you like negative attacks? Do you like criticism? Do you like gossip and malice and dirt?' and they say no, they're lying."

Television news was also criticized for the way it covers the economy. "This is serious because the presidency was won and lost on the economy," one member declared. "Some economic news is actually good news . . . but the story is always 'economic indicators are up, but. . . . '" A television news executive agreed: "The argument can be made that it was probably more important how the networks and the major newspapers covered the economy during the campaign than anything we said about the campaign. . . . There is something worrisome about how every time a statistic comes out we say it, but then have to say, 'on the other hand. . . . '"A reporter offered an explanation for this phenomenon. "It's because we don't understand economics," he said. "There is a historic tendency in journalism to have reporters separate from economic reporters. They are believed to wear strange undergarments or something. . . . Economic reporters never become anything else, yet you can be a specialist in the atomic bomb and end up anywhere."

The discussion ended on that note. As happened in the first two meetings, while the Task Force reached consensus in identifying many problems facing television coverage of presidential campaigns, little time was left for more detailed discussions of specific recommendations.

BACKGROUND PAPERS

BY

KATHLEEN HALL JAMIESON
KEN AULETTA
THOMAS E. PATTERSON

THE SUBVERSIVE EFFECTS OF A FOCUS ON STRATEGY IN NEWS COVERAGE OF PRESIDENTIAL CAMPAIGNS

KATHLEEN HALL JAMIESON

Since news reporters tend to see events through symbolically significant moments, let me open with what I regard as the most revealing moment of the 1992 primary campaign.

In the three days before the New York primary, talk-show host Phil Donahue turned his attention to the campaign. Of Jerry Brown, he asked, "You went to Africa with Linda Ronstadt. Did you go anywhere else with anybody else?" Donahue's questions of Bill Clinton focused on whether the Arkansan had or hadn't had affairs.

Midway through Donahue's assault on Clinton, an exasperated candidate and an audience member both said, "Enough!" To rising audience applause Clinton added, "We're going to sit here a long time in silence, Phil. I'm not going to answer any more of these questions. I've answered 'em until I'm blue in the face. You are responsible for the cynicism in this country. You don't want to talk about the real issues." As the crowd voiced its approval, an audience member agreed. "Given the pathetic state of most of the United States at this point . . .," she said, "I can't believe you spent half an hour of airtime attacking this man's character. I'm not even a Bill Clinton supporter, but I think this is ridiculous!"

In penance, Donahue devoted his last show before the New York primary to an uninterrupted discussion between Democratic contenders Jerry Brown and Bill Clinton. The worst of times had given way to the best. The exchange proved as substantive as any in the campaign, and more civil. And it reached an audience not usually attracted by PBS and C-SPAN.

Those three days on "Donahue" raise the questions Whither? and Whether?

Every four years of the last twenty, scholars of political communication have complained that the press coverage of campaigns has offered little substance and too much strategy. If the press were to do a better job, goes the argument, campaigns would have greater relevance to governance. We would have known in 1964, for example, that Lyndon Johnson would take us into a full-scale land war in Vietnam and in 1968 that Richard Nixon would not get us out. We would have seen in 1972 that Nixon was indeed a crook, in 1976 that Jimmy Carter had neither a vision nor a realizable plan, and in 1980 that Reaganomics was "voodoo economics." And in 1988 we would have grappled with the S and L crisis. Lost in sorties against the press, of course, is the realization that the candidates, the public, and the educational system figure prominently in the problem, as well.

I don't mean to suggest that scholars simply recycle the same old set of complaints. The demands of tenure require more. In 1972, the key finding said that voters learn more from ads than from news. In 1980, the indictments centered on the evils of polls. After 1984, the press-academic axis asked, "Was the so-called character issue blunting the political aspirations of those most qualified to lead?" In 1988, ad pollution was the dominant complaint: "Not enough 'substance.'" "Too much on the trivial; too little on the significant." And discussing the primaries of 1992, the custodians of the democratic ideal said, "Too much on 'Gennifer with a G' and 'How could he not have inhaled?'; too little on comparative records on the environment, job creation, and relative dispositions to compromise."

With the predictability of the swallow, journalists have responded that they report what is there to report. Vacuous campaigns produce vapid coverage. They have noted, as well, that scholars make sense of campaigns over months or years, whereas reporters usually have a matter of hours. Besides, when the press offers substance—as the major newspapers have in their scrutiny of H. Ross Perot, as PBS does with "Frontline," "MacNeil/Lehrer," and Bill Moyers, as ABC does with "Nightline," as CBS, NBC, and ABC do with their Sunday interview shows, as CNN is doing with its Markle programming, as all of the networks did in sponsoring the 1992 primary debates—the public yawns and turns to "The Simpsons," HBO, or reruns. Nineteen-ninety-two has proven no exception. By any reasonable standard, viewership for the primary debates was low.

Still, after each of the last twenty years' presidential campaigns, reporters have sworn allegiance to an unrealized and, some would say, unrealizable ideal. "We shall do better" is the chorus that emerges from the seemingly nonstop debriefings on the campaigns. We gather to commemorate the beginning of another quadrennial cycle of sin and repentance, scapegoating, guilt and expurgation.

In this working paper, I shall try to step beyond the stock academic indictments to ask what it is about contemporary presidential campaigns that every four years produces another cycle of failed aspirations on the part of reporters and frustrated expectations among academics and average folks. I will suggest that a focus on strategy is difficult to dislodge because the culturally familiar language of sports provides a coherent way to process campaign data. I will argue that strategy coverage and use of polls have fused in ways that shape the "who, what, and how" of coverage. I will suggest that the unholy alliance between strategy coverage and polls minimizes rather than enhances the learning that can occur from presidential debates, and has created a strong tendency in reporting not simply to magnify the effectiveness of political ads but to create ads in news. Finally, I will suggest that the 1992 campaign demonstrates that the press can break from the strategy perspective. Specifically, the press deserves high praise for its recent monitoring of campaign ads.

Much of the material in this working paper is drawn from two books: *Presidential Debates: The Challenge of Creating an Informed Electorate* (New York: Oxford, 1988) which I coauthored with David Birdsell in 1988, and *Dirty Politics: Deception, Distraction, and Democracy* (New York: Oxford, 1992).

THE FOCUS ON STRATEGY, GAME PLAN, HORSERACE

"We celebrated Roger Ailes for his craft as a maker of television ads that created a picture of Michael Dukakis as a friend of murderers and rapists," recalled *New York Times* columnist Anthony Lewis in late November 1988. "There were lots of stories about the superiority of the technicians on that side: value-free stories. . . . I do not think the press should be cheering the corrupters for their efficiency."[1]

As rhetorical theorist Kenneth Burke observes, as "we are using language, it is using us."[2] The language through which the press reports on politics assumes that the American electorate selects a president through a process called a "campaign" seen as a "game" or "war" between a "front-runner" and an "underdog" in which each "candidate's" goal is "winning." Candidates' words and actions are seen as their choice of what they presumably consider a means to victory. So enmeshed is the vocabulary of horserace and war in our thoughts about politics that we are not conscious that the "race" is a metaphor and "spectatorship" an inappropriate role for the electorate. Press reliance on the language of strategy reduces candidate and public accountability.

A schema is a cognitive structure through which we process events or information. So, for example, we share a "restaurant schema," which leads us to assume that upon arrival at a restaurant we will be seated, be offered a menu, order, and then receive a check. In my book *Dirty Politics:*

Deception, Distraction, and Democracy I argue that the press invites the public to see politics through a strategy schema.

In the strategy schema, candidates are seen as performers, reporters
as theatrical critics, the audience as spectators. The goal of the per-
former is to "win" the votes of the electorate, projected throughout the
performance in polls. The polls determine whether the candidate will
be cast as front-runner or underdog, whether the candidate will be
described as achieving goals or "trying" to achieve them, and how the
candidate's staged and unstaged activities will be interpreted. In the
strategy schema, candidates do not address problems with solutions,
but "issues" with "strategies." The language of the strategy schema is that
of sports and war. This vocabulary lets reporters, candidates, and the public ask, "Who is winning, and how?" The posture invited of the electorate
by this schema is cynical and detached.

The storyline of the strategy schema encourages voters to ask not
"Who is better able to serve as president?" but "Who is going to win?"
"Winning and losing are presented as all-important," writes political scientist Doris Graber, "rather than what winning and losing mean in terms
of the political direction of the country in general or the observer's personal situation in particular. Taking its cues from the media, the audience
accepts election news as just another story rather than as an important
tale that will directly affect its own welfare in real life."[3]

News coverage "primes" or "cues" viewers and readers to see, store,
and analyze "campaigns" through the strategy schema. The results are
reflected in the way voters talk about campaigns. So, for example, political scientist Thomas Patterson found that in 1976 the "game" was the
subject of voter conversation more often than were the substantive
elements of the campaign.[4] When 106 focus-group respondents in a total
of nine states[5] were asked weekly for twelve weeks of the 1990 general
election to list what, if anything, they had learned about their statewide
campaigns in the past week from watching local and national news, 73
percent of the responses dealt with campaign strategy or who was where
in the polls and why.

Why the focus on strategy? Increasingly, scholars agree with an explanation offered by political scientists Michael Robinson and Margaret
Sheehan. "For a host of reasons, objective journalism has, for a century and a half, defined news as *events*, as happenings," note Robinson
and Sheehan. "'Horse races' happen; 'horse races' are themselves filled
with specific actions. Policy issues, on the other hand, do not happen;
they merely exist. Substance has no events; issues generally remain stat-
ic. So policy issues, or substance, have been traditionally defined as outside the orbit of real news."[6]

Other factors come into play as well. Strategy was the native tongue
of those reporters who once were campaign insiders. In 1988 the guild

of former campaigners now covering campaigns included ABC's Jeff Greenfield, NBC's Ken Bode, CBS's Diane Sawyer, CNN's Pat Buchanan, ABC's George Will, MacNeil/Lehrer's David Gergen (also of *U.S. News & World Report*), NBC News vice president Timothy Russert, and independent producer Bill Moyers (most frequently seen on PBS). Chris Matthews, the Washington Bureau Chief for the *San Francisco Examiner*, is former press secretary to Democratic House Speaker Tip O'Neill. In 1988 he doubled as a regular political consultant appearing on CBS News, as did Representative Jack Kemp's former press secretary, John Buckley. Syndicated columnists Jody Powell and William Safire also led earlier lives in presidential service.

The revolving door turned both ways. Reporters who gave up pen or mike for government appointments carried into the bureaucracy an insider's understanding of how the news could be shaped. The first presidential campaign to carry large numbers of reporters and producers into candidate service was Nixon's in 1968. Patrick Buchanan had been an editorial writer for the St. Louis *Globe-Democrat;* Ray Price had performed the same function for the New York *Herald Tribune.* Nixon's television advisers in 1968 included Frank Shakespeare, formerly a CBS vice president, and Roger Ailes, formerly of the "Mike Douglas Show." Nixon's 1968 campaign communication coordinator was a former *Time* magazine editor, James Keogh.

Following the lead of Theodore White, whose *Making of the President* series reshaped journalists' conception of the available means of story construction, many of the nation's top reporters envisioned the campaign year ending with a best-selling book answering the question "Who won, and how?" Their titles reveal the strategy schema simmering below the story line: *Portrait of an Election*, by Elizabeth Drew; *Marathon: The Pursuit of the Presidency, 1972–1976*, by Jules Witcover; *Dasher: The Roots and Rising of Jimmy Carter*, by James Wooten; *The Road to the White House*, by a team from the *New York Times*; *The Quest for the Presidency: The 1988 Campaign*, by Peter Goldman, Tom Mathews, and the *Newsweek* Special Election Team; *The Winning of the White House 1988*, by the editors of *Time* magazine; *Road Show*, by Roger Smith.

Alongside these are the more arcane works of those of us who call the university home. Like reporters, academics reinterpret the polls, analyze how the campaign agendas were formed, and account for the strategies behind the candidates' use of news, advertising, and the debates.

In 1988 there were "10 national polling organizations in the field, and a new poll was reported every second day on average during the final months of the campaign."[7] During the 1988 primaries, nearly a third of the network news election stories made note of poll results.[8]

Pollsters are augurs. What they forecast is victory or defeat. These prophecies determine how reporters treat the candidate. "Coverage of candidates and their campaigns differs qualitatively depending on their relative standing [in the polls]," writes Democratic pollster Harrison Hickman. "Stories about candidates doing well in polls usually focus on what they are doing *correctly*—the policy positions, campaign strategies, and personal qualities that put them at the top of the preference rankings. Coverage of candidates doing badly in polls usually focuses on what they are doing *wrong*—various factors that put them behind front-runners." [9]

Words are outward signs instituted by polls to determine place. In the primaries, the amount of news space or time a candidate receives is a function of standing in the polls; the symbolic moments chosen to stand for the campaign as a whole are determined in part by the reporters' reading of the polls' divinations. Among other things, this means that candidates ahead in the polls are more likely to see segments of their ads run in news to illustrate the effectiveness of their communication strategies. Polls also shape the nouns, verbs, and adverbs that reporters choose to characterize a candidate's discourse and behavior.

The strategy schema assumes that candidates' expressions of caring, the stressed features of their biographies, and the problems and solutions they offer are all the calculated product of strategic choice. Those who believe that the candidates are motivated by selfless conviction see reports framed by the strategy schema as cynical invitations to public cynicism. Those who believe that candidates are consummate sophists see strategy reports as realistic revelations of the fundamental machiavellianism of those who seek public office.

The cynicism, suggest reporters, is in the campaigns and in the electorate. "To appeal to an increasingly alienated electorate," writes the *Washington Post*'s E. J. Dionne, "candidates and their political consultants have adopted a cynical stance which, they believe with good reason, plays into popular cynicism about politics and thus wins them votes."[10]

While that is undoubtedly true as far as it goes, the cynicism is in the reporting as well. Refusing to take candidates' words and actions as anything other than crass ploys to influence votes invites public cynicism. Even if pandering is the intent of candidates, their words entail commitments for which they will be held accountable once elected, and as such should be treated seriously. Whether the Star Wars Initiative was promoted or opposed by the president made a difference in how tax dollars were used, for example. And no one seriously doubts that Walter Mondale and Michael Dukakis would have placed different justices on the Supreme Court, with palpable differences in human lives, than did Ronald Reagan and George Bush. There are practical differences that do matter. Treating campaigns as little more than meaningless posturing tends to obscure these differences.

If reporters believed that candidates were saying things of importance to the nation, why would they instead use precious news time to ask about polls? Not only do polls distort, but they distract as well. "In Philadelphia, Bush went to mass with Cardinal John Krol," noted ABC's Mike Von Fremd (October 30, 1988). "And while he was posing for cameras, enjoying the autumn breeze, it was clear that things weren't quite falling into place. The Vice President was asked if his internal polls that show his lead is slipping are right." Bush answered, "One, I don't think they are. And two, I'm not going to say any more about it." In late October, Sam Donaldson noted of Dukakis, "But even if people are listening to what he says now, the polls show he's still losing ground. Are you depressed about the polls, Governor?" Dukakis replied: "Feel good, feel good, Sam." "How can you, sir?" asked Donaldson. "Things go well," said the Democrat. Donaldson then observed, "Candidates who appear to be losing can't quit"(October 26, 1988). The polls have both generated and capped this story segment.

The strategy schema is problematic because it disengages the electorate from the election and minimizes the accountability of the candidates in seven ways. First, the electorate can know who is ahead, why, and what strategies are necessary for each to win, without knowing what problems face the country and which candidate can better address them in office. The strategy schema asks questions which position its audience as campaign consultants, not knowledgeable voters.

Second, the strategy schema invites audiences to critique a campaign as if it were a theatrical performance in which the audience is involved only as spectators. It asks whether candidates "seem," "look," "appear" presidential, whether their strategies are coherent, resonant, and unobtrusive; and whether they are running an effective campaign. Once we have answered these questions and hence drawn a reasonable inference about who will win, the strategy schema invites us to no further involvement in the campaign.

Third, the strategy schema displaces such questions as "Is the candidate's rhetoric, including speeches, ads, statements in debates, and statements by surrogates, fair, accurate, and relevant to governance?"

Fourth, the strategy schema minimizes the educational value of a campaign's most informative moments, those that occur in mass exposure to general-election presidential debates. Blinded by the strategy schema, reporters reduce debate coverage to three questions: who won? why? and what impact will the debate "performance" have on the outcome of the election? This constricted focus on unanswerable and silly questions reduces the panorama of information gathered by all segments of the viewing public to irrelevant data.

Fifth, the strategy schema invites voters to trust presumed experts rather than themselves. It is "experts" who conduct and interpret the meaning of polls, "experts" who tell us who "won" and "lost" debates, "experts" who evaluate the strategic successes and failures of the candidates. Reliance on experts reduces the personal accountability of the viewing, reading, listening, thinking voter. Reliance on experts certified in news increases our vulnerability to other forms of "expertise," such as that carried by the unseen announcer in political ads.

Sixth, reliance on the strategy schema means that campaigns are shifting from communication to metacommunication, thereby reducing the informational content available to voters.

Seventh, the strategy schema is cynical. It takes nothing at face value. Its world is Machiavellian. And since it assumes that both candidates are pandering sophists, it minimizes the disposition of the press to elicit, or of the viewer to discern, the important differences the candidates would bring to the process of governance.

The strategy focus takes time and space that could be spent dispensing richer information. At the same time, shifting from the strategy schema does not necessarily sacrifice the useful information voters garner from it. A performance/promise or problem/solution focus would require that reporters be prepared to cover issues not focused on by the candidates and to try to get the candidates to address them as well. The press focus on strategy means that reporters are more likely to concentrate on the issues on which the candidates focus in speeches, ads, and debates than on those treated only in passing (as was our changed relations with the Soviet Union in 1988) or ignored (as, for the most part, was the emerging S and L crisis in that campaign). So, for example, what the members of the "Moscow intelligentsia" who are experts at the U.S.A. Institute noticed about the 1988 presidential campaign was "neither the personalities of the candidates nor their tactics, but what had been ignored or evaded. This was the issue the Soviet policymakers believed was central, and it consumed them night and day. The issue was the ending of the Cold War."[11]

Strategy coverage does little to help the country confront what conservative theorist Kevin Phillips describes as "a critical weakness in American politics and governance . . . the frightening inability of the nation's leaders to face, much less define and debate, the unprecedented problems and opportunities facing the country."[12]

COVERAGE OF ADS AND THE CREATION OF ADS IN NEWS AND LIVE TALK SHOWS

On September 4, 1991, CBS, NBC, ABC, and CNN news stories all carried an excerpt from a conservative Victory Committee ad urging Senate confirmation of Supreme Court nominee Clarence Thomas and attacking the integrity of his likely opponents, including one who was not even on the Senate Judiciary Committee.

As a result, viewers saw and heard content they would not otherwise have been exposed to on these news programs. "Who will judge the judge?" asked a segment of the ad. "How many of these liberal Democrats could themselves pass ethical scrutiny?" (Pictures of Alan Cranston, Joseph Biden, and Edward Kennedy are shown.) As the charges unfold, they are repeated in print on the screen. "Ted Kennedy, suspended from Harvard for cheating, left the scene of the accident at Chappaquiddick where Mary Jo Kopechne died." (A headline from the *Washington Star* appears.) "And this year Palm Beach." (On screen, a photo of the front page of the *New York Post* showing a picture of Kennedy in casual wear and the headline "Teddy's Sexy Romp.") "Joseph Biden, found guilty of plagiarism during his presidential campaign. Alan Cranston, implicated in the 'Keating Five' S and L scandal. Whose values should be on the Supreme Court? Clarence Thomas's or Ted Kennedy's?" (The headline "Teddy's Sexy Romp" with the attached photo is juxtaposed with a photo of Thomas.)

With the exception of CNN's "Crossfire," the news broadcasts did not focus on the accuracy or fairness of the attacks but rather on the potential impact of the campaign on the Thomas hearings. A small conservative group with a membership of 80,000 had managed to garner over a million dollars' worth of network time with an ad that cost $20,000 to produce and just under $40,000 to air on Fox and CNN in the Washington, D.C., area.

In the process of relaying the controversial segments of the ad to their viewers, the networks legitimized the unsupported inference that Kennedy had either engaged in questionable sexual behavior or, worse, was an accomplice in the alleged rape of a young woman by his nephew at the Kennedy Palm Beach home. The headline came from the *New York Post*. It referred to a later discredited report that Kennedy, wearing only an undershirt, had chased a young woman around the Palm Beach residence. As corrected, the report revealed that the senator had simply appeared in a living room in which a young woman was talking with Kennedy's son. The senator was at the time wearing a nightshirt that went down to his knees.

As the controversy about the ad raged, the *New York Times* ran a still from the ad on its front page.

Although in 1991 the local print press in Louisiana tipped its coverage against the gubernatorial candidate it consistently identified as a former Klansman and Nazi sympathizer, the national broadcast media built audiences and ratings by providing David Duke one opportunity after another to telecast newsads to the folks back home. As a result, by November 13, 58 percent of a national sample could correctly identify Duke; only 30 percent could identify his opponent Edwin Edwards.[13] That meant that Duke had wider name recognition than any of the declared Democratic candidates for president!

Duke transformed free national airtime on such shows as "Good Morning America," "Today," "Crossfire," "Donahue," "Nightwatch," "Nightline," and "Larry King Live" into national "newsads" (free news exposure that closely resembles the context of a political ad) for his statewide candidacy. While Edwards was on the air in Louisiana in paid time, Duke was using national interview time to beam ads of his own back home. Twice during his interview on CNN's "Larry King Live" and once on "Nightline," Duke urged viewers to write for more information or to send contributions to his Louisiana headquarters. On "Larry King Live," Duke gave the address including zip code. National publicity helps account for the fact that four out of ten of Duke's contributions came from outside Louisiana.[14] Without a single national direct-mail effort, Duke managed to receive contributions from every state in the Union other than Rhode Island, North and South Dakota, and Alaska![15]

Not only did Duke make appeals for support but he also used national interview time to insinuate false claims into public consciousness. Unchallenged on either "Larry King Live" or "Nightline" was Duke's assertion that the U.S. Post Office lowers the test scores of whites and raises them for blacks. A spokesperson for the U.S. Post Office categorically denies that statement, saying that the only score alterations are for veterans, who receive an extra five points, with disabled veterans receiving ten.

On the Larry King show, Duke declared that he had letters from billion-dollar-a-year companies eager to come to Louisiana if he were elected; King asked for evidence. The letter Duke read was not from a company wanting to bring jobs to Louisiana but from a bond company that wanted Louisiana's business! King never questioned the supposed evidence.

Duke demonstrated repeatedly that he could use national television for his purposes. Before agreeing to appear on "Donahue," he elicited a commitment from the host not to use the visual capacity of television to make an attack ad out of his appearances. To get Duke to appear, Donahue agreed not to show photos of him in Klan regalia and not to print on the screen statements he had since disavowed. When Duke told a "Donahue" caller, "I'm here in the lion's den," he had little to fear. His prior agreement had bearded the lion.

In each of the nationally televised interviews, Duke's tone was earnest, his demeanor restrained, his voice modulated, his language polite and filled with "Sir" and "Ma'am." As a result, he sounded and looked more like a talk-show host than a Hitler or a Huey Long. Had earlier photos and news clips been shown, they would both have bonded Duke to his disclaimed past and asserted visually that his cosmetic transformation was more visible than his Christian one. The Louisiana Coalition against Racism and Nazism was highlighting the visual contrast in full-page ads showing "before" and "after" pictures of Duke under the headline "Some Change Is Only Skin Deep." "He changed his face," said the print ad. "He changed his political image. But he can't change the truth."[16]

More important, earlier clips showed a "hot," intense, more stereotypically demagogic style. The visual and tonal contrast between Duke's Klansman past and Christian present raises more powerfully than words can the question "Who is the real David Duke?" and with it the suspicion that there is more to Duke than meets the eye.

Duke's use of "Larry King Live" and "Donahue" forecast similar uses by independent presidential candidate H. Ross Perot, who effectively launched his presidential bid on King's show.

PROTECTIONS FROM FALSE ADS

Three protections stand between the voter and ad pollution: candidate use of free time, candidate use of paid time, and the protections that come from an electorate able to secure information from sources other than ads. Two of these require the help of the press. Using free time against paid time usually means that the attacked candidate responds to the false ad at a press conference clipped into broadcast and print news, or in a telecast debate. While of some value, reliance on news and debates entails three problems. First, the audiences for ads and these two other forms differ. Far more people see political ads than watch debates, digest a daily newspaper, or spend dinner with Peter Jennings. Additionally, a debate or news piece will respond to the questionable ad once, while the ad itself can air many times; repetition gives the ad a natural advantage. Moreover, news and debates tend to use words as their weapons. In the contest between evocative pictures and spoken words, pictures usually win. Finally, news coverage has more often been part of the problem than part of the solution. Most newscasts in 1988 magnified the power of false advertising rather than minimizing it.

Candidate debates provide an opportunity for one candidate to hold another accountable for the claims found in the ads. In 1984 Walter Mondale used this opportunity effectively in the New York primary when he turned to his opponent Gary Hart in a debate and asked why he was saying in his ads that Mondale favored killing kids in Central America. And one characteristic of the 1992 primary debates was the candidates' use of them to unmask false charges in their opponents' ads.

The second protection is a well-informed electorate. For a number of reasons that protection isn't working. In a nutshell, citizens under the age of thirty are now less likely to read a newspaper than are their parents and grandparents. And the electorate as a whole spends little time with the substantive fare found on the "MacNeil/Lehrer NewsHour," in the "Frontline" documentaries, and on C-SPAN.

Still, there are things the press can do for those willing to attend. We should expect the press to note violations of the consultants' own "Code of Professional Ethics." In it, they pledge that they will "use no appeal to voters which is based on racism or discrimination and will condemn those who use such practices . . . will refrain from false and misleading attacks on an opponent or member of his family and shall do everything in my power to prevent others from using such tactics . . . will document accurately and fully any criticism for an opponent or his record . . . [and] shall be honest in my relationship with the press and candidly answer questions when I have the authority to do so."[17]

We also can support the "citizen jury" concept pioneered in 1990 by the Minnesota League of Women Voters. A revivified form of the Fair Campaign Practices Commission, the juries involve representative citizens from around a state eliciting candidate positions and holding candidates accountable for the responsibility and accuracy of their claims.

The National Association of Broadcasters has urged stations to reject unfair or inaccurate ads brought to them by political action committees. Interested citizens can remind stations of the NAB position and reiterate the fact that stations are under no obligation to air PAC ads and can be sued over misrepresentations found in them. Candidates whose records are distorted in PAC ads then should sue both the airing station and the PAC. Such action should encourage stations to exercise greater vigilance in screening these ads.

A dozen and a half states now have on their books laws governing campaign conduct. Some govern only claims about an opponent; others (e.g., Minnesota and Massachusetts) include claims candidates make about themselves. In most instances these laws were enacted as part of the state's corrupt practices act. Wisconsin, both Dakotas, Utah, and Oregon are among the states whose statutes permit removal of a guilty official from office. Interested citizens should encourage their states to enact such statutes and encourage the responsible officials to enforce the law.

The process would be well served if candidates were voluntarily to accept the recommendation of nationally syndicated columnist David Broder that soon after an ad begins airing, the sponsoring candidate take questions on its content and accuracy. Consultants should be expected to air their ads for the press and to make available documentation for the ad's claims. In 1990, for the first time, most major consultants made such information available, in response to the rise of "ad watches" in newspapers and on television stations.

I have serious reservations about the constitutionality and wisdom of the Clean Campaign Act of 1985, also known as the Danforth-Hollings

Bill. This bill would require candidates to appear in their own attack ads and would provide response time for those attacked. It would counterbalance PAC and private third-party ads by giving the opposed candidate free response time, thereby providing an incentive for stations to reject all noncandidate ads. The difficulty with this proposal is its built-in bias toward already well funded incumbents; most oppositional ads are produced for less well funded challengers. At the same time, it would raise thorny questions about what does and does not constitute an attack.

DEBATE COVERAGE

Empaneled or not, reporters play a central role in presidential debates. As rhetorical theorist Robert Scott argues, press coverage about whether Jimmy Carter would or would not debate created expectations that disadvantaged the incumbent when such a debate finally occurred. By forecasting a Carter who would be tough, incisive, and a master of detail, press accounts heightened Carter's vulnerability when he instead appeared stiff and ill at ease. By making the fairness of ducking debates an issue, by painting Carter as one who sought advantage in excluding John Anderson, press coverage created a scenario in which "it was simple enough to perceive Reagan as long-suffering; denied an early confrontation with Carter through his insistence on being fair to John Anderson and finally granted a face-to-face encounter only when and under conditions that seemed upon the surface to favor Mr. Carter." Within the debate itself "pushing hard to put Reagan on the defensive, Carter fulfilled the prophecy of the press. His efforts looked strategic because they had been so labeled well in advance for instant identification. . . . Carter's very presence in the debate after standing aloof the first time, as well as his hard struggling, underscored beliefs like Tom Wicker's wicked depiction of his 'hard won reputation for indecision, ineptitude and speed on the backtrack.'"[18]

As its part of the equation, the press would cover the substance of debates as well as candidates' strategies. If broadcasters opened a debate with a summary of the candidates' already stated positions, the electorate would be better served. analyses should begin by summarizing the similarities and differences between the candidates, and then indicate what was added to that knowledge by the clash of the debate. "What did we learn?" not "How, if at all, did they blunder?" would be the central question asked by broadcasters.

Since reliance on print to correct errors and clarify discussion does little to educate those who do not read newspapers, we need to find a way to move information now carried in print to the broadcast media and then to tie it to the analysis of the debate itself. "You can say anything you want during a debate," observed George Bush's press secretary in 1984, "and 80 million people see it." But when reporters demonstrate that a candidate misinformed, "so what? . . . Maybe 200 people read it, or 2,000 or 20,000."[19]

To inform the 80 million debate viewers requires that the national broadcast news channels do as the best newspapers have done and correct misstatement of fact, clarify points of ambiguity, and point to nonanswers. There is no reason that the networks cannot follow the pattern Jim Wooten of ABC set in 1988 and analyze debate inaccuracies on the news the next evening. This process would be eagerly aided by the campaigns, which in the past three presidential elections have assembled research teams to control the spin on news reports. In the clash of competing claims about who lied about what, reporters can locate some of the areas worthy of public clarification.

Reporters should also abandon the win-lose mentality that pervades coverage of debates. At the minimum, the possibility that both candidates have won should be considered. After all, the esteem in which most viewers hold both candidates rises after each debate. Occasionally, the campaign insiders concede as much: A team of Carter's 1976 advisers concluded that those debates "helped both candidates by diminishing, if not eradicating, the general public's negative perceptions of each."[20]

More important, "winning" is in large part not a function of actual performance in the debate but is the byproduct of audience predispositions. We tend to distort the positions of the candidates we favor and posit more agreement with them than we actually share. So, for example, in 1980 Carter's supporters magnified their agreement with Carter, and Reagan's supporters did the same with Reagan.

An ideal debate model presupposes a disinterested audience able to act as an impartial judge swayed by the merits of one case rather than another. Instead, the audiences for debates turn on their television sets primed to see their favored candidate vindicate their belief in his or her competence and virtue. Accordingly, 82 percent of those who supported Reagan for president in 1980 thought he had won the debate with Carter; 69 percent of Carter's supporters disagreed, believing that their candidate had done the better job.

If the supporters of one candidate are more likely than those of the other to watch the debate, then national surveys reveal little other than which candidate had the larger number of viewing partisans. This was the case for Reagan in 1980, when 86 percent of his supporters and 81 percent of Carter's watched the debate. The CBS/Associated Press poll gave Reagan the debate, by 44 percent to to Carter's 36 percent. Had a larger number of Carter's supporters been watching, the results would have been closer.

The tendency to view Reagan as the winner was magnified by ABC's use of a methodologically flawed telephone survey to assess outcome. "Probably the most influential post-debate event was the telephone call-in conducted by ABC," recalled Reagan debate adviser Myles Martel. "Although Carter's aides were quick to assail its methodology—and justifiably so—tens of millions of Americans saw Reagan outdistancing Carter in the poll by a 2 to 1 margin before they turned off their television sets. Additional millions of voters were exposed to lead stories about these results the following morning in the newspapers and on television news programs."[21]

The sample of callers who paid for a call to ABC was self-selected. The fact that it cost money to call undoubtedly discouraged the poorer Democratic constituency. Since ideologues are more likely to engage in active communication behavior, the response could also indicate that Reagan's supporters felt more strongly about him than Carter's did about him—a rating on intensity, not an accurate representation of total support. We know from a Harris survey that Reagan's supporters were more intensely partisan than Carter's.

These facts of political behavior led communication scholars Leuthold and Valentine to postulate three principles governing perception of who won a debate:

1. The candidate with the most supporters in the debate audience is likely to be considered the winner, all other things being equal. This means that a candidate with a substantial lead in the polls is likely to be considered the winner, and to profit the most, if he performs as well as his opponent.

2. If the numbers of supporters of each candidate are equal, the candidate with the most intense supporters is likely to be considered the winner. The intense supporters will be more likely to watch and to declare their candidate the winner.

3. If the numbers of supporters are equal, the conservative Republican candidate is likely to be declared the winner, because his conservative Republican supporters will be more active, and this activity will include watching the debates and declaring their candidate the winner.[22]

The notion that we can immediately know who had made the best case should also be suspended. Initial appearances can deceive. As Edwin Yoder, Jr., of the *Washington Post* observed in 1984, Reagan at first appeared to many to be the winner: "Responses were deft, and brilliantly crafted for the limited attention level of television." Yet when analyzed carefully after the debate, Reagan instead seemed "underinformed and imprecise about vital matters of detail."[23] Support for Yoder's observation comes from an unlikely source: After watching the Reagan-Carter debate, Reagan's pollster Richard Wirthlin concluded that Reagan had won. When he read the transcript, he observed, "Thank God it was on television."[24]

WHOSE LANGUAGE IS THIS?

Critics from Coleridge to Kenneth Burke have recognized the power of naming. For Coleridge, a word doesn't "convey merely what a certain thing is, but the very passion and all the circumstances which were conceived as constituting the perception of the thing by the person who used the word."[25] One might paraphrase Burke to say that language does our thinking for us.[26] Note, for example, the different perspective invited by calling an action the "Grenada incursion" rather than the "Grenada invasion," and by terming U.S. and allied actions the "Gulf War" rather than the "Oil War" or the "War for the Sheiks." Along similar lines, one might argue that if the perspective of one campaign infuses the vocabulary of reporters, that candidate has obtained a significant advantage.

Whereas in earlier political campaigns, one side or the other occasionally enticed the press into embracing one of its words or phrases, in 1988 the Bush campaign managed to insinuate an entire vocabulary about the campaign into press coverage. The reporting on the Dukakis record on crime is illustrative. Here the Republicans secured the complicity of the press in renaming convicted murderer William Horton, in redefining the relationship between Horton's Maryland victims, in adopting such words as "torture" and "terrorize" to describe his actions while on furlough, in defining the furlough program's purpose as dispensing "weekend passes," and in talking of the policy as a "revolving door." Each of these acts of naming biased the discussion against Dukakis. Each was inaccurate. To the extent that the Republicans were able to set this language in place, however, they demonstrated the power of ads, reinforced by candidate speeches, and campaign hype, to contextualize news.

Although his given name is William, he calls himself William, court records cite him as William, a July 1988 *Reader's Digest* article identifies him as William J. Horton, Jr.,[27] and press reports prior to the Republican ad and speech blitz name him "William," the Bush campaign and its supporting PACs identified the furloughed convict as "Willie" Horton. Even the crusading anti-Dukakis newspaper that won a Pulitzer Prize for its exposé on the furlough program consistently identifies Horton as William Horton or William Horton, Jr. When the Maryland man who was stabbed by the furloughed convict contacted the *Lawrence Eagle-Tribune*, he too referred to Horton as William Horton.[28] In his account of the attack in the PAC ad, however, that man, Clifford Barnes, instead identifies the convict as "Willie" Horton.

One might trace the familiar "Willie" to the naming practices of slave-masters, to our patterns of talk about gangsters, or to the sort of benign paternalism that afflicts adults around small children. But whatever its origin, in discussions of murder, kidnapping, and rape, "Willie" summons more sinister images of criminality than does "William." After all, it wasn't J. "Eddie" Hoover who hunted down "Alphonse" Capone. And during his trial, the person to that point known as Willie Smith was identified by family and attorney as either William or Will. After his acquittal on charges of rape, the family reverted to the name by which he had been known before the trial.

The televised PAC ad titled "Weekend Prison Passes," as well as the PAC ads featuring Horton's victims, all refer to him as "*Willie* Horton." When his mug shot appears on the screen of "Weekend Prison Passes," the name under it reads "Willie Horton." Reporters reduced Dukakis on crime to the Republican sculpted image of "Willie Horton." In news reports, "*Willie*" Horton's name was mentioned more often by reporters than by George Bush or any of his representatives. Use of dramatic, coherent narrative increases the likelihood of recall.[29] Once the Horton narrative was embedded in public consciousness, mention of his name should have been sufficient to evoke the entire story.

By the campaign's end, even the Democratic candidates had accepted the Republican identification of Horton (Lloyd Bentsen interview with Dan Rather, October 26, 1988; Dukakis interview with Rather, October 27, 1988; Dukakis interview with Peter Jennings, November 9, 1988). The most prominent exception occurred before Horton became a stock feature in Bush's stump speech and the subject of PAC ads. In the *Washington Post* of July 8, 1988, Richard Cohen wrote about "*William* Horton's Furlough."

The schizophrenic labeling of the *New York Times* seemed to invite a Woody Allen to shout that the czar and the tsar were the same person. An editorial on June 30, 1988, labels Horton "Willie Horton." Yet pieces by Robin Toner on July 5 and Martin Tolchin on October 12 refer to him as "William R. Horton." In Tolchin's article, it is Clifford Barnes who identifies Horton as "Willie Horton."[30] The difference between the two sets of articles appears to be that "Willie Horton" is written about by anonymous reporters tasked with inside reporting and given filler space. By contrast, "issue" pieces carrying bylines write of "William Horton." The contrast raises the unconfirmed possibility that the more contact a reporter had with Bush campaign insiders, the more likely the use of "Willie." The assumption falters on the editorial presumably written by someone safely anchored to a desk in New York.

The press adopted the phrases "weekend furloughs" and "weekend passes" from the Republican speeches and ads, which in turn located them in the *Lawrence Eagle-Tribune*. The phrases are inaccurate. Furloughs in Massachusetts ranged from 1 hour to 74 hours in 1987 and from 1 hour to 170 hours in 1986,[31] and furloughs could be granted for any day or days of the week. In 1987, the median number of hours of leave per furlough was 19, 5 hours less than a full day and 29 less than a weekend. Horton's approved 48-hour furlough began on Friday, June 6, 1986, which means he should have returned to prison while most of us were still enjoying what we usually define as a weekend.

Bush reinforced the notion that these were weekend events by averring that he says to criminals, "Make my day!" while Dukakis says, "Have a nice weekend!" "Weekend" suggests that the furloughs occur frequently, when in fact in 1988, as in 1986, a prisoner was permitted no furloughs for the first half of his or her sentence and in 1988 could be furloughed only in the final three years before eligibility for parole or release.[32] As of April 1988 furloughs were ended for anyone who ever was a first-degree murderer not eligible for parole.

Weekend is a time for recreation and leisure. This association suggests that the assault and rapes were leisure activities for the prisoners. Bush suggested as much when he called on in his audience to ask Dukakis why he had let "murderers out on vacation" (June 1988 speech to Illinois Republican Convention in Springfield).

The Bush furlough ad is titled "Revolving Door" and speaks of Dukakis's "revolving-door prison policy." Although the visual in the ad itself shows not a revolving door but a turnstile, reporters also adopted the Republican announcer's characterization of the program as a "revolving-door" policy. So, for example, Dan Rather asked Lloyd Bentsen, Democratic vice-presidential nominee: "Can't a person, or can a person, be deeply concerned about *revolving-door* justice and laxity toward criminals, even when the criminal happens to be someone who is black, and still not be a racist?" (CBS Evening News, October 26, 1988).

In describing the ad, reporters adopted the Bush language as well. So, for example, in an article examining inaccuracies in the ads of both campaigns, the *Washington Post*'s Lloyd Grove writes "another Bush campaign commercial featuring hard-eyed men in prison garb streaming through a *revolving door*" (*Washington Post*, October 31, 1988, p. A8).

Despite the use of the words "turnstile" or "gate" in all questions to our Texas focus groups, 36 percent of the respondents referred to the furlough ad as the "revolving door ad."[33]

Here is an instance of the complexity of the visual-verbal relationship. The repeated use of the phrase "revolving door" couples with repeated viewing of the image of the circling actors as convicts to establish the visual-verbal link in memory. "Revolving door" also suggests a frequency and casualness in the administration of the furlough program that did not characterize the Massachusetts system.

From PAC ads made by Horton's victims, reporters adopted the words "slashed," "brutally," "terrorized," and "tortured." "For twelve hours I was beaten, slashed, and terrorized," says Clifford Barnes, "and my wife Angie was brutally raped." "Horton went on to rape and torture others," says the sister of the man killed by Horton. Bush helped set the language in place. On June 24, he stated, "In no other state would a cold-blooded murderer like *Willie* Horton have been set free to *terrorize* innocent people."

"Slashed," "terrorized," and "tortured" are not the words usually used by reporters to characterize crime. Nor was it the language first used by the national press to describe Horton's actions. On December 2, 1987, before the furloughs became a campaign issue, CBS aired a segment that "took a hard look today at a standard procedure for many of the nation's prisons. Forty-five states," said Dan Rather, "offer furlough programs which release inmates from prison for limited times to see how they handle freedom." The language of the correspondent is the factual, calm, descriptive language characteristic of crime reporting in network news. "William Horton did strike again in this Maryland house where Cliff and Angela Barnes lived. He held them hostage for twelve hours. Horton raped her twice, tied her husband up in the basement and stabbed him twenty-two times." But by June 26 and July 20, CBS reporters Jacqueline Adams and Lesley Stahl were calling Horton "Willie" and adopting the tabloid-like language of "torture" and "terror."

Once the Republican language was in place, it became the optic through which the press saw, and invited us to see, Horton's actions. The *Washington Post* favored the word "terrorized" (October 22, 1988; October 25, 1988; June 23, 1988, "terror"), as did columnist Tom Wicker (*New York Times*, June 24, 1988). CBS reports ran the full range from "brutally" (Jacqueline Adams, June 26, 1988) to "savagely" (Bob Schieffer, October 7, 1988). *Newsweek* preferred to label "*Willie* Horton" "the Massachusetts murderer who *tortured* a Maryland couple" (October 31, 1988, p. 16). The *New York Times*, which on July 5 described "William Horton" as "a convicted murderer" who "broke into the couple's home, bound and stabbed Mr. Barnes and raped his wife," by mid-October had "*Willie* Horton" "viciously" attacking and also adopted Barnes's word "*slashed* with a knife" (*New York Times*, October 10, 1988, "Convict's Victim Makes an Ad"). NBC's Lisa Myers adopted the word "tortured" (October 24, 1988). On October 24, 1988, on the "MacNeil/Lehrer NewsHour," Kwame Holman noted, "Cliff Barnes was *tortured* with a knife for twelve hours and *his wife*, Angela, was raped twice by *William* Horton, an escapee from the Massachusetts prison furlough program."

Academics embraced the Republican language as well. "The furlough program was emphasized," writes journalism professor David Myers, "because *Willie* Horton, a black man who had been convicted of first-degree murder, had escaped to Maryland on a *weekend pass*, where he *brutalized* a white man and raped his fiancée."[34]

As interesting is the fact that when offered two different constructions of the relationship of the couple assaulted by Horton, until late in the campaign the press adopted the more incendiary of the two. At the time of the Horton attack, Clifford Barnes and his fiancée were living together. The first PAC ad to air on the topic says accurately that Horton "kidnapped a young couple, stabbing the man and repeatedly [twice] raping his *girlfriend*."[35] That ad began airing September 9. On October 20 a second PAC ad was aired in California. This spot features Clifford Barnes, who is now married to the woman who was his fiancée at the time of the attack by Horton. "My wife Angie was brutally raped," says Barnes.

The sources that identify Angie as Barnes's wife at the time of the attack include CBS (December 1987), Cohen in the *Washington Post*, Holman of "MacNeil/Lehrer," and Toner in the *New York Times*. Although in an October 23, 1988 report, ABC's Joe Bergantino identifies Barnes as her "boyfriend," two days later ABC's Britt Hume identifies Barnes as her "husband." On NBC, on October 28, this identification was reinforced in what I elsewhere define as a "newsad," a segment of news that might as well have been paid candidate advertising:

> Ken Bode: George Bush was here [California] again today, again talking about crime.
>
> Bush: I believe in safe neighborhoods, and I say I believe it is time for America to take back our streets.
>
> Bode: Like everywhere else, the Democrats have been on the defensive about crime. Willie Horton's victims made a campaign commercial.
>
> Cliff Barnes in ad clip: For twelve hours I was beaten, slashed, and terrorized, and my wife Angie was brutally raped.
>
> Bode: But mostly, Bush's tough talk on crime works, because it fits with what Californians see on their news each day.
>
> Man: When you have gang murders in the headlines, day after day, I think the voters understand that there is only one candidate in this race who is truly tough on crime. Only one candidate for president who really supports the death penalty.

The Republicans' use of Horton shaped the visual portrayal of crime in network news in ways that reinforced the mistaken assumption that violent crime is disproportionately committed by blacks, disproportionately committed by black perpetrators against white victims, and disproportionately the activity of black males against white females. In other words, the Republicans' use of Horton shaped the visuals in 1988 network crime coverage in a way that underscored the Bush message.

James Devitt and I have systematically examined the ways in which alleged criminals were portrayed in network news from 1985 to 1989. In 911 scenes of alleged criminals in 530 network news stories, blacks were proportionately more likely than whites to be shown restrained and in actual mug shots—the two visuals shown in the Horton PAC ads. Robert Entman has found the same pattern in local news.[36]

I suspect that this disproportionate exposure to black males in mug shots increases the telegraphic power of the use of the Horton mug shot in the PAC ads. This finding raises the question, What subtle chain of inferences or visceral responses might be invited by Senator Jesse Helms's showing of a close-up still photo of his opponent Harvey Gantt?

Our data also provide a baseline telling us about how often blacks are likely to appear as "alleged criminals" in news and what visual forms this representation will take. By comparing the appearance of blacks as alleged criminals in crime stories from 1985 to 1989 with their appearance in stories about the issue of crime in the 1988 general election, we can determine whether the crime stories of 1988 differed significantly from contemporary norms. They do. The increase in the proportion of blacks identified or shown as criminals in 1988 general-election stories about crime is statistically significant. The number of female victims per news story doubled in the 1988 stories about Horton.

Just as the Bush campaign verbally primed reporters' discussion of crime, so too the issue of Horton subtly primed producers and editors to include more blacks in their covering shots showing presumed criminals. The most egregious example occurred on ABC on October 31, 1988. The reporter was Ken Kashiwahara. All of the presumed criminals but one were black or Hispanic. All of those who said they were afraid were white, and most were women.

To portray as a typical criminal a black male who was an accessory to a felony murder, assaulted a white male, and raped a white female is inaccurate. Blacks run a greater risk of forcible rape, robbery, and aggravated assault than whites. Low-income individuals are the most likely victims of violent crime. Men are more likely than women to be the victims of violence.[37] FBI statistics confirm that, unlike robbery, rape and murder in the United States are primarily intraracial, not interracial, phenomena. In 1988, for example, only 11.3 percent of the reported rapes involved a black rapist and a white victim.[38]

I do not intend to minimize Thomas and Mary Edsall's claims that a higher percent of the crime committed by blacks is interracial and that in the categories of assault and robbery more than half of the robberies committed by blacks have white victims.[39] Rather, my point is that raising the fear of whites that they are likely to be murdered or raped by blacks is unjustified. Identifying William Horton's actions as somehow typical, as George Bush did in his speeches, is racist.

Moreover, a disproportionate portrayal of blacks as criminals plays on racial fears. When network news segments on crime visually cast blacks in disproportion as criminals, the news stories themselves are priming both a pro-Bush and a racist response.

If candidates' ability to shape news coverage was the news of 1988, the news of 1992 is the ability of candidates to bypass news entirely. The reason: the rise of talk radio and television.

The emergence of the talk show as a site of both substance and silliness suggests a system in transition. By providing callers and audience members with direct access to candidates, the format enfranchises. Participation rather than spectatorship is invited by its interactive form. Moreover, it attracts an audience otherwise largely inaccessible to candidates.

But because the hosts range from dedicated partisans to entertaining lightweights, a skillful candidate can transform many of these opportunities into "interview ads" or "newsads." And while callers ask useful and often important questions, most are unskilled in follow-up. The opportunity to ask a second question is usually not provided, in any event. In other words, while potentially productive, the talk-show form is not likely, of itself, to elicit a high level of argument, engagement, and accountability.

AND NOW FOR THE GOOD NEWS

We can encourage public rejection of unfair discourse by applauding reporters, papers, and stations that offer fact-based, not strategy-based, ad watches. We also should encourage newspapers and television stations to editorialize against false ads. The *Washington Post* demonstrated the power of a strong, clear, recurrent editorial voice when it faced down the National Rifle Association with a series of strong editorials supporting gun control in Maryland.

In three instances in the recent past—in Pennsylvania, Georgia, and Texas—the vigilance of the broadcast and print press has protected the public from distortive political advertising.

Thornburgh–Wofford in Pennsylvania. The Thornburgh–Wofford U.S. Senate race was notable not simply for Harris Wofford's focus on national health insurance but also for his success in countering Richard Thornburgh's questionable ads. What made this possible was a vigilant press, a sophisticated ad team that let no untruth go unrebutted, and a campaign with the financial wherewithal to get the rebuttals on the air.

The Wofford response ads drew credibility from press coverage of Thornburgh's and Wofford's claims. In fall 1991, the press in Pennsylvania monitored the Wofford–Thornburgh Senate race in Pennsylvania more carefully and with clearer effect than any other Senate race in recent memory. In both Pittsburgh and Philadelphia, the major papers checked the candidates' "facts," set claims in historical context, and exposed sins of both omission and commission in political ads and speeches. So, for example, when Thornburgh claimed that Wofford's national health-care plan would cost 300,000 Pennsylvanians their jobs or have "other severe impacts," reporters contacted the two authors of the study Thornburgh had cited. They had not seen the Wofford plan. Their study of the Kennedy and Mitchell plans did not necessarily generalize to Wofford's, reported the two. Thornburgh's claim and the authors' denial were carried throughout the state. When Wofford attacked Thornburgh for spending taxpayers' money for a "junket" to Hawaii, the papers corrected the claim by noting that Thornburgh had delivered a speech that fell within his duties as attorney general, and had remained on the island only a few hours.

The state's major newspapers, as well as the *New York Times*, checked the accuracy of the claims in ads. "You decide," said an early Thornburgh ad. "Dick Thornburgh was a highly acclaimed prosecutor. Harris Wofford was a liberal-college president who led the school to big budget deficits." Reporters asked the Thornburgh campaign for proof and sought out confirmation from the president of Bryn Mawr College, Mary Patterson McPherson, who disputed the Republican claim and documented a reduction in the school's indebtedness under Wofford. "Each year from 1972 to 1978, he added to the college endowment," she stated.[40] The *Philadelphia Daily News* asked Thornburgh's camp for documentation and reported that even Thornburgh's data show "Bryn Mawr's deficit shrinking, both in size and as a percentage of the budget, during Wofford's tenure."[41]

Wofford's counteradvertising and the vigilance of the press turned the race into "Truth or Consequences." "While my opponent was Governor Casey's Secretary of Labor and Industry," said Republican Richard Thornburgh on the stump and in his ads, "the number of people out of work increased by 100,000." By contrast, while he was governor, Thornburgh noted, the state had added 500,000 new jobs. "Neither Mr. Thornburgh nor his advertisement mentioned that about 400,000 manufacturing jobs were lost in Mr. Thornburgh's administration," noted an article in the *New York Times*, "or that unemployment almost reached 15 percent at the height of the 1982 recession in his first term."[42] On similar grounds, the *Philadelphia Inquirer* found both campaigns doctoring their claims about jobs and joblessness.

Another Republican ad said: "Adnan Kashoggi. Notorious big arms dealer. What kind of man would solicit money from him? Harris Wofford." The facts? In 1977, when Wofford was president of Bryn Mawr College, Kashoggi tried to establish a Middle Eastern Studies department at Bryn Mawr, Swarthmore, and Haverford. When a student-faculty committee recommended that the school accept money only for purposes that Kashoggi couldn't influence, such as scholarships and books, Kashoggi withdrew the offer.

On October 31, 1991, the *Philadelphia Inquirer* editorialized against that ad. "Our candidate for the worst negative ad . . . ? The thirty-second Thornburgh [ad] that laughably strains" to link Wofford to "notorious big arms dealer" Adnan Kashoggi. "'Late hit' doesn't begin to describe it. This is an ad from another planet." The Pittsburgh papers joined in the condemnation.

"What the newspapers said enabled us to blunt any negative attack by Thornburgh," said Wofford strategist Bob Shrum. "We could use what the papers said about the Kashoggi ad to blunt any other negative attack. If they would make that claim, they would be willing to say anything. That ad was so far over the line that I think the papers would have editorialized against it even if they hadn't been doing ad watches."

Buchanan–Bush in the Georgia Primary. In the 1992 Georgia primary, voters surprised those who had assumed that the South surfeits with "Bubbas" eager to vote their prejudices by penalizing Republican hopeful Patrick Buchanan for an unfair attack on incumbent president George Bush.

With scenes from the film *Tongues Untied* as the backdrop, print scrolled up the screen proclaiming: "In the past three years the Bush Administration has invested our tax dollars in pornographic and blasphemous art, too shocking to show. This so-called art has glorified homosexuality, exploited children, and perverted the image of Jesus Christ. Even after good people protested, Bush continued to fund this kind of art."

The broadcast media helped discredit the tale of a president funding pornography. On CNN (February 28, 1992), Brooks Jackson pointed out that the film had been funded by the Reagan, not the Bush, administration at a total cost to the taxpayers of $5,000. NBC's Lisa Myers went a step further (March 3, 1992) to note that the film was not typical of National Endowment for the Arts projects.

As she made this claim, Myers displaced the ad's images with shots of the Chicago Symphony and Pavarotti on PBS. These, she argued, were more representative of the endowment's mission and expenditures. Both NBC and CNN distanced audiences from the ad by boxing it on the screen and dampened the power of the ad's visuals by imposing the words "misleading" or "false" over the ad copy in appropriate places.

Thirty voters in three Georgia focus groups had been selected because the demographics of the groups matched those of the state and because they were undecided three weeks before the primary. The night before balloting, each group was asked whether the Buchanan ad had made them more or less likely to support Buchanan or hadn't changed their inclination at all. Seven said that the ad had made them less likely to support the Republican insurgent. A week after the balloting in Georgia, a CNN-Gallup poll confirmed that the NEA ad had created a backlash against Buchanan. Indeed, 23 percent said that the ad had increased the likelihood that they would vote for Buchanan's opponent, George Bush.

Richards–Williams in Texas. Under the caption "KVUE 24 Truth Tests," Carol Kneeland at the Austin station took a Clayton Williams ad to task for "doubling the state budget to claim government had grown by more than it had." Williams pulled the ad.

Although he did not withdraw the ad, Ann Richards's media adviser, Bob Squier, was cited for "distorting a newspaper headline by leaving off words attributing to her its negative comments about her opponent." To avoid a repeat of that embarrassing incident, Squier now compares all headlines in ads to the original.

As interesting is Kneeland's claim that the ad watch helped rather than hurt the station economically: "More than one candidate said they bought more time on our station because they thought the Truth Tests were attracting more politically aware viewers to our newscasts." The focus on facticity in the candidates' ads and speeches displaced the kind of strategy coverage that drives academics to distraction. "We avoided the horserace stories about who's ahead, who's behind, and what's the latest campaign strategy, the stuff journalists and campaign insiders find fascinating," Kneeland says, "but which is not all revealing to a voter trying to decide how to vote based on issues and character."[43]

NOTES

1. Frank E. Gannett Lecture, Washington, D.C., November 28, 1988.

2. Blankenship, *Political Science Quarterly*, 314.

3. Doris Graber, *Mass Media and American Politics,* 3d ed. (Washington, D.C.: Congressional Quarterly, 1989), p. 221.

4. Thomas E. Patterson, *The Mass Media Election* (New York: Praeger, 1980), p. 105.

5. See Kathleen Hall Jamieson, *Dirty Politics*, p. 303.

6. Michael J. Robinson and Margaret A. Sheehan, *Over the Wire and on TV: CBS and UPI in Campaign '80* (New York: Russell Sage Foundation, 1983), p. 148.

7. P. Meyer, "Precision Journalism and the 1988 U.S. Election," *International Journal of Public Opinion Research* 1 (1989): 195–205. Quote is on p. 196.

8. Robert Lichter, Daniel Amundson, and Richard Noyes, *The Video Campaign: Network Coverage of the 1988 Primaries* (Washington, D.C.: American Enterprise Institute, 1988), p. 65.

9. Harrison Hickman, "Public Polls and Election Participants," in *Polling and Presidential Election Coverage*, ed. Paul J. Lavrakas and Jack K. Holley (Newbury Park, Calif.: Sage, Inc., 1991), p. 101.

10. E. J. Dionne, *Why Americans Hate Politics* (New York: Simon & Schuster, 1991), p. 17.

11. Sidney Blumenthal, *Pledging Allegiance: The Last Campaign of the Cold War* (New York: HarperCollins, 1990), p. 3.

12. Kevin Phillips, *The Politics of Rich and Poor: Wealth and the American Electorate in the Reagan Aftermath* (New York: Random House, 1990), p. ix.

13. The survey was conducted by the Wirthlin Group and reported in the *Times-Picayune*, November 13, 1991, p. A11.

14. Tyler Bridges, "Loss Isn't the End for Duke," *Times-Picayune*, November 17, 1991, p. A6.

15. "Edwards Money from La.," *Times-Picayune*, November 25, 1991, p. A12.

16. *Times-Picayune*, November 3, 1991, p. A39. I thank Professors Kathleen Turner and James Mackin of Tulane University for their assistance in gathering materials on this race.

17. Code of Professional Ethics of the American Association of Political Consultants, 1989.

18. Robert L. Scott, "You Cannot Not Debate," *Speaker and Gavel* 18 (1981): 32.

19. Kathleen Hall Jamieson and David S. Birdsell, *Presidential Debates* (New York: Oxford, 1988), p. 215.

20. Ibid.

21. Myles Martel, "Debate Preparation in the Reagan Camp: An Insider's View," *Speaker and Gavel* 18 (1981): 45.

22. D.A. Leuthold and D.C. Valentine, "How Reagan 'Won' the Cleveland Debate: Audience Predispositions and Presidential debate 'Winners,'" *Speaker and Gavel* 18 (1981): 65–6.

23. Nationally syndicated column, October 24, 1984.

24. In Joel Swerdlow, ed., *Presidential Debates 1988 and Beyond* (Washington, D.C.: Congressional Quarterly, 1987), p. 45.

25. Samuel Taylor Coleridge, *Shakespeare Criticism*, ed. Middleton Raysor (London: Dutton, 1907).

26. Cf. Kenneth Burke, *The Philosophy of Literary Form*, 3d ed. (Berkeley: University of California Press, 1973), p. 3 ff.

27. Robert James Bidinotto, "Getting Away with Murder," *Reader's Digest* 133 (July 1988): 57–63.

28. Susan Forrest, "How 12 Hours Shattered Two Lives," *Lawrence Eagle-Tribune*, August 16, 1987.

29. See N. S. Johnson and J. M. Mandler, "A Tale of Two Structures: Underlying and Surface Forms in Stories," *Poetics* 9 (1980): 51–86.

30. Editorial, "Furloughs from Common Sense," *New York Times*, June 30, 1988, p. A22; Robin Toner, "Prison Furloughs in Massachusetts Threaten Dukakis Record on Crime," *New York Times*, July 5, 1988, p. B5.

31. "1987 Annual Statistical Report of the Furlough Program," Massachusetts Department of Correction, December 1988, p. 6.

32. Massachusetts' Correctional System Document 103CMR-157, February 2, 1990, p. 3.

33. For a discussion of focus group findings, see Chapter 1 of *Dirty Politics*. For uses of "revolving door" see Gerald Boyd, "Bush's Attack on Crime Appeals to the Emotions," *New York Times*, October 11, 1988, p. 12: "In addition, Mr. Bush's campaign has aired television commercials that portray the prison system in Massachusetts, where Mr. Dukakis is the Governor, as a revolving door that releases inmates on weekend passes,"; Gerald Boyd, "Despite Vow to be 'Gentler,' Bush Strays on Attack," *New York Times*, October 29, 1988, p. 8: "Mr. Fuller said that although Mr. Bush hoped to end the campaign on a 'positive note,' there were no plans to remove television commercials like that which accuses Mr. Dukakis of operating the Massachusetts prison program as a 'revolving door.'"

34. David Myers, in *The Media in the 1984 and 1988 Presidential Campaigns*, ed. Guido H. Stempel III and John W. Windhauser (New York: Greenwood Press, 1991), p. 169. Note the tacit assumption that because the man is white, his fiancée must be white as well.

35. "Weekend Prison Passes," produced by Larry McCarthy for Americans for Bush.

36. For our results, see *Dirty Politics*. pp.133–34. Robert Entman, "Modern Racism and the Images of Blacks in Local Television News," *Critical Studies in Mass Communication* 7(4) (December 1990): 332–45.

37. *Sourcebook*, 1988, 298, table 3.17.

38. *Criminal Victimization in the United States*, 1988, U.S. Department of Justice, NCJ-122024, December 1990, table 43.

39. Thomas Byrne Edsall and Mary D. Edsall, *Chain Reaction: The Impact of Race, Rights, and Taxes on American Politics* (New York: W. W. Norton, 1991), p. 236.

40. "Campaign Hotline," October 15, 1991, p.13.

41. Quoted in ibid.

42. Michael deCourcy Hinds, "Ads and Attacks Rise in Pennsylvania Senate Race," *New York Times*, November 1, 1991, p. A19.

43. Quoted in *Dirty Politics*, p. 159.

ON AND OFF THE BUS:

LESSONS FROM CAMPAIGN '92

KEN AULETTA

L ike a hive of agitated insects, reporters stalked Bill Clinton in New Hampshire, swarming around him in such numbers that often you couldn't see the Democratic presidential aspirant. What you heard was the buzz of mindless insider questions—"Will you stay in the race if you lose the New Hampshire primary?" "Are you angry?" "Are you encouraged by the polls?" "Do you expect your opponents to pick on you in tomorrow's debate?"

It was mid-February 1992, and the questions had actually improved. Weeks earlier, serious reporters first apologized and then asked: "Did you ever sleep with Gennifer Flowers?" Even CNN, which generally distinguished itself this season, succumbed to the mindless hysteria by interrupting its regular coverage to carry Gennifer Flowers's January 27 press conference live. It was easier for the four Democrats competing against Clinton in the February 18 New Hampshire primary to stroll a street unnoticed than it was for Baltimore *Sun* columnist Jack Germond, whose face had become so familiar to viewers of CNN and "McLaughlin & Co." Desperate for attention, the four contenders lay awake devising sound-bite tricks—"MTV news," Republican strategist Roger Ailes dubs it—to divert attention from Clinton. "We just spent two and one-half hours preparing for the debate tonight and one-half hour of it was on substance and two hours was spent on coming up with snappy one-liners!" said Michael McCurry, senior adviser to Senator Bob Kerrey of Nebraska. Everyone remembered how Ronald Reagan jump-started his faltering candidacy in 1980 by grabbing the microphone in a New Hampshire debate and bellowing, "I've paid for this, Mr. Bush."

    Kerrey and Tom Harkin and Paul Tsongas and Jerry Brown fretted
about Clinton, but on the eve of the nation's first primary, the governor of Arkansas knew his main foe was the media, the hive of reporters
interposing itself between him and the voters. He knew he had to
escape the incessant questions about Gennifer Flowers and her impact
on the polls, escape questions about how he had eluded the military draft
three decades ago. He had to get back to talking about the economy, to
showing that he was not a slick, draft-dodging male bimbo. So Clinton
struggled to bypass the media middleman. Twice he purchased a half-
hour on local TV to take direct questions from viewers. His staff distributed
twenty-thousand video tapes to voters. He appeared at rallies all over the
state. Clinton was determined to meet some voters.
    He did not always succeed. He was trapped in a new version of a
familiar pastime: the Political Insider Game. Novelist and essayist Joan
Didion, who dropped in on the 1988 presidential campaign as if she were
visiting another planet, wrote this in the November 1988 *New York
Review of Books:*

> When we talk about the process, then, we are talking, increas-
> ingly, not about "the democratic process," or the gener-
> al mechanism affording the citizens of a state a voice in
> its affairs, but the reverse: a mechanism seen as so spe-
> cialized that access to it is correctly limited to its own pro-
> fessionals, to those who manage policy and those who
> report on it, to those who run the polls and those who
> quote them, to those who ask and those who answer the
> questions on the Sunday shows, to the media consultants,
> to the columnists, to the issues advisors, to those who give
> the off-the-record breakfasts and to those who attend them;
> to that handful of insiders who invent, year in and year
> out, the narrative of public life. . . . What strikes one most
> vividly about such a campaign is precisely its remoteness
> from the actual life of the country.

    Throughout the first half of the 1992 contest, the rules of this
game were pretty much established by the "boys on the bus," by the established press which had supplanted the political parties as the filter (bro-
ker) between candidate and voter. The press's power had grown expo-
nentially since 1970, when the Democratic party (soon followed by the
Republicans) amended their rules, allowing primaries or caucuses of reg-
istered voters to replace party elders in choosing candidates. These
rules were supposed to usher in a new era of direct democracy. Instead,
the media substituted for party bosses. It became the responsibility of
the media to screen the candidates—to inspect their character, their

charisma, their competence, their skills, their electability—particularly during the crucial year before voters had their say.

This the media imperfectly prepared to do. Prior to the primaries, we had few objective measures of how candidates were faring. We had too little intimacy or shared history with them, didn't know how to distinguish between their public and private character. We too rarely dwelled on public policy or what candidates might actually do as president. We lacked the tools to do this. Or television lacked the pictures. Or we were terrified of boring our readers or viewers. Or maybe we didn't want to bore ourselves.

Usually, we feasted on politics as an end in itself, not a means to a governmental end. We defined news as what was fresh, which meant we did not mine the candidates' basic stump speech or themes because we had heard it all a zillion times before. We searched for drama, conflict. In the words of Kathleen Hall Jamieson, dean of the Annenberg School for Communication at the University of Pennsylvania, we treated the candidates "as performers, reporters as theatrical critics, the audience as spectators." We announced who staged the best events, who looked smooth, who sounded good, who had the sharpest attack, who was winning—who gave the best performance. Not surprisingly, one result of this insider game was shrinking voter turnout.

Another result was an era of press celebrities. With celebrity came guest appearances on "This Week with David Brinkley" and "Capital Gang" and "McLaughlin & Co." and "Meet the Press" and all the other pundit programs that lead to lucrative lecture fees and require only that the pundit have opinions that can be compressed into a sharp sound bite. The trick to join this Press Insider Gang and play in the game is to be the all-knowing handicapper.

Playing this game further estranges the press from the public for at least three reasons. First, what reporters are supposed to do is ask questions, which presupposes humility. The questions are to be asked by people who don't think they already know the answer. But what inevitably happens to "stars" is that they lose their humility. They prefer being asked questions. Second, performers don't enhance the popularity of the media. "Jack Germond is an old friend, and I've said to him many times that he should not be on a show like McLaughlin's," says David Broder of the *Washington Post*. "It cheapens journalism. It gives people the impression that what political reporters do is stand around and holler at each other." Finally, shows like these frame what a troubled Germond calls the "instant wisdom," setting the tone—the politically correct posture—for much of the media.

The "boys on the bus" framed Act One—let's call it Pre-Perot—of the presidential contest, which ran from May 1991 to February of 1992. When former senator Paul Tsongas was first to announce his candidacy in May 1991, only three dozen reporters journeyed to Lowell, Massachusetts, to witness it. When Tsongas went to Iowa, the BBC and Dutch journalists tagged along, but no members of the regular press gang, remembers an incredulous Peggy Connelly, his press secretary. In the parlance of insiders, Tsongas was deemed an also-ran, as were Harkin and Brown and Kerrey and Wilder and even Clinton, whose October announcement speech was covered live by CNN but interrupted in mid-sentence just as he began to specify what he might do as president. CNN broke away to a studio where two of its knowledgeable pundits, David Broder and William Schneider, handicapped the race. Insiders believed the thoroughbreds had yet to enter the contest. Watch out for Cuomo, they said. He'd chase all but one or two contenders from the fray.

But who would be Cuomo's challenger? At first, the sages generally thought it would be Kerrey. Then they cooled on him, said he lacked a coherent message. Clinton then caught their eye. They noticed his boldness in attacking potential vulnerabilities. To combat rumors about his personal life, Clinton brought Hillary along to Godfrey Sperling's regular breakfast of media heavies in Washington in September, where he volunteered that their union "has not been perfect" but they had worked through the difficulties. The sachems of the press were impressed. He was shrewd, said Germond, to say this and to vow not to answer any demeaning "have you ever"—Gotcha!—questions. Clinton had staged a preemptive strike, much as Mrs. Jesse Jackson had in 1988 when she admonished reporters to refrain from trying to dig up dirt to "destroy my family."

Then when Clinton wowed an Illinois gathering of Democratic state chairs on November 23, word filtered out from the thirty or so national reporters in attendance: Clinton's the one. Alone among the field, he had honed a message, mastered the issues, crafted the best applause lines, chiseled an efficient campaign and fundraising apparatus. He seemed to have thought most deeply about how to avoid the pitfalls of Dukakis, Mondale, Carter, McGovern, or Humphrey, the Democratic candidates who had lost five of the past six presidential races.

Oh, but President Bush still had a 70 percent approval rating in the fall of 1991. Insiders chimed that Bush was a shoo-in. By the winter of 1992, they heralded Pat Buchanan as a stronger foe than he turned out to be. By spring, the instant insider wisdom was that Bush would clobber any foe, particularly Clinton. By summer, they would chime that Bush was a has-been.

What intruded on the prognostications of insiders were the "feeding frenzies" unleashed by the local press and by newspaper and TV tabloids— by outsiders. Such behavior was usually frowned upon by the established press, even as they paused to clear their throats in order to describe the significance of the frenzy and its political fallout. Sometimes, insiders joined in the frenzies themselves. A frenzy could be frightening. They were moments, said Clinton's communications director, George Stephanopoulos, as he watched the hive blanket his candidate in Manchester, New Hampshire, when "individuals are transformed into an organism. . . . I think of the press like the Congress. I like all of them individually, but not as a group." The group dynamic, observed *Washington Post* reporter David Von Drehl, is one of conformity: "If everyone else has it and you don't go with it, then it looks like you're covering up. That's when the critical mass loses its mind."

What was new about the first big frenzy of 1992 was that it was sparked by outsiders. This year, it wasn't provoked by the "boys on the bus"— by the regular press contingent that, straining for the perfect metaphor, cornered George Romney after he said he was "brainwashed" by American generals in 1968, or pursued Jimmy Carter for saying he was attacked by a "killer rabbit" (1979). The spark wasn't lit by the *Wall Street Journal,* which wormed into Geraldine Ferraro's family finances in 1984; nor by the *Miami Herald,* which staked out Gary Hart's home in 1987; nor by *Newsweek,* which in 1988 first printed rumors (and a family denial) about an alleged Bush mistress.

No, this year noninsiders—the national *Star,* syndicated TV shows like "A Current Affair" and "Hard Copy," tabloid newspapers, and local TV news—were the spark. They established the peer pressure. They set the pace. And they did it by relying more on rumor than reported fact.

The frenzied behavior of the press helped provoke Act Two, which opened in the first quarter of 1992. If what the candidates said in Act One was essentially filtered by the media, then Act Two featured an attempt by the candidates to circumvent the media middleman and reach voters directly.

In doing this, the candidates were catching up with and riding a wave. Everywhere, citizens strive to decentralize government and eliminate middlemen. The wave washed over socialist governments in Eastern Europe. It arrived with TV clickers and multiple channel choices that permit viewers to bypass the Big Three networks and program for themselves. It's happened with mail-order catalogues or computers that allow customers to shop or bank at home. It's happened with discount chains like Wal-Mart and The Gap. It's happened with corporations that shed layers of management so that workers are closer to their product. And so it happened in 1992 when candidates and citizens alike rebelled against the media middleman. This year they decoded— perhaps forever, perhaps ominously—the insider game once dominated by the "boys on the bus."

◆ ◆ ◆

Whereas the press performed a familiar middleman role throughout 1991, this time the media started out more humbly. After a woeful press performance in 1988, a cascade of studies gushed forth, all designed to awaken better coverage. Among others, the Kettering Foundation warned that voters were alienated by a system run by political and press insiders. The Joan Shorenstein Barone Center at Harvard urged news organizations to develop their own plans to cover the campaign and, in a separate report, called on CBS, ABC, NBC, CNN, PBS, and C-SPAN to devote ninety minutes of nine Sunday evenings for substantive conversations and debates with the candidates.

This year the press was determined to be less reactive. Most news organizations began planning their campaign coverage early, determined to downplay the too familiar horserace and character coverage and to play up the real issues. "Motion and thought tend to be enemies," said Ron Brownstein of the *Los Angeles Times*, explaining why he like other reporters often opted to stay off the campaign bus and broaden their bank of sources to include academics and "people of thought." This year, agreed Paul Friedman, executive producer of ABC's "World News Tonight," correspondents were rotated more and allowed to roam from the campaign "cocoon," they were less consumed by photo opportunities, and greater efforts were made to decipher what was true or false when a candidate made sweeping claims in either a debate or an advertisement.

This year the four national TV news networks, the *New York Times*, the *Wall Street Journal*, and much of the press conscientiously tried to explore not just issues but the precepts and public character of the men seeking the highest office. But, alas, other factors intruded, at least initially. Partly because of the recession, partly because politics smells like fish to most consumers, and partly because the accountants had more leverage, less time and space were devoted to it this year. From Labor Day through January 1992, said the Tyndall Report, which monitors television, the networks earmarked "58 percent less coverage" than was true for the same period during the 1988 contest. Because of budget constraints, the networks—like the newsweeklies—did not assign a reporter to each candidate; instead the networks relied on young associate producers to tail each candidate through the winter of 1992. If the networks needed a picture, often they now relied on local stations.

This year what was truly different were the local cameras. "What's happened this time," says David Broder, the respected dean of national reporters who has covered every presidential contest since 1960, "is that not so much the networks as the locals are asserting themselves. You can really see the effects of the economic problems on the networks. They are not creating the same clot as they used to. I can recall times when there would be three crews from the same network at a single event."

The emergence of local television was reflected in another way. This year the candidates more aggressively used technology to disseminate their message. Starting with President Bush and a New Hampshire station in January, the candidates used satellites to conduct live interviews with local stations around the country. During the primary season, reports the Freedom Forum Media Studies Center at Columbia University, twice as many local stations used satellite interviews in 1992 as was true in 1988; and partly to save money, one in ten local stations now accepted video news releases produced by the candidate—a threefold increase over 1988—with half failing "to reveal the source of this material to viewers."

Still, the essential truth about Act One of this campaign was that the "boys on the bus" still set the rules of the game. By November 1991, the Press Gang had decided that Bob Kerrey was probably too unfocused—too existential a character—to be a candidate-warrior. So in mid-November, when Kerrey whispered what he thought was a private (if lame) joke about Jerry Brown to an open microphone, the established media pounced on this as a metaphor for the "aimless" Kerrey campaign, just as crying symbolized a supposedly "volatile" Muskie in 1972.

Kerrey's joke precipitated the first mini-feeding frenzy of the contest. Kerrey attracted headlines, and a major Clinton economic-policy speech became an asterisk. This conformed to what Bush adviser Roger Ailes has called his "orchestra pit" theory of politics: "If you have two guys on a stage and one guy says, 'I have a solution to the Middle East problem,' and the other guy falls in the orchestra pit, who do you think is going to be on the evening news?"

In January, the story line became: Clinton's the front-runner. Before a vote was cast, and even though polls showed that more than half of all rank-and-file Democrats didn't even know who he was, Clinton was hailed on the covers of *Time*, the *New Republic*, and *New York* magazine. "I argued against doing a cover at that time," said *Time*'s national political correspondent, Laurence I. Barrett. "But I was not at all unhappy with what the cover story said. It was a balanced, professional job." The January 27 *Time* cover did not win the same plaudits from colleagues. A June 1992 *Times-Mirror* poll of more than four hundred political reporters and editors found that of those who recalled it, twice as many reacted negatively as positively. Admittedly, there is a blurred line between promoting a candidacy, as critics think *Time*, *New York*, and the *New Republic* were doing, and making legitimate news that Bill Clinton, through dint of effort, was coming on strong. When R. W. Apple first reported from Iowa in early 1976 that a peanut farmer and former governor from Georgia was poised to pull an upset in party caucuses, he was celebrated for brilliant reporting. What was similar in Carter's and Clinton's case, however, was this: the press was the sole scorekeeper and the public mere spectators in what Thomas B. Rosenstiel of the *Los Angeles Times* dubbed "the shadow primary phenomenon."

While Clinton was helped by the media, President Bush was hurt by it. In January, polls showed the president's approval ratings had sunk from over 70 to 53 percent. A survey of TV coverage conducted by the Center for Media and Public Affairs in Washington concluded: Bush "got the worst press (only 28% positive)." Even Buchanan fared nearly twice as well. The story line was that Bush's January 28 State of the Union address was a critical juncture, a test of his "vision." It was an expectations contest whose outcome was largely determined by a speech, by style. Bush beat the game in 1988 with his demagogic "Read my lips" speech to the Republican convention. But this year it was a game the president would lose.

The media as filter was stamped on the first of seven planned prime-time presidential debates, this one on NBC in mid-December. Anchor Tom Brokaw, an astute student of politics, stood as the candidates sat, looking like schoolboys. Brokaw paced in front of them, asking questions. Because there were so many candidates, each was allotted only a minute to respond to his queries. Unavoidably, the anchorman was the only person on stage invested with authority.

In another debate just prior to the New Hampshire primary, moderator Cokie Roberts, like Brokaw, alone asked the questions. Many of her questions, like Brokaw's, were intelligent, but the candidates thought they detected in them a familiar journalistic smirk. Bob Kerrey thought Roberts's questions were designed more to snare "a good story"—to play Gotcha!—than to tell voters what they "need to know," particularly when she asked: As President, would you sign New Jersey's welfare reform bill? "That's not a question people care a damn about," said Kerrey. "The question was asked incorrectly. It wasn't asked in a way to allow us to debate welfare. The right question is: 'What's wrong with welfare?' or 'Why are so many black children born out of wedlock?'"

Playing Gotcha! is neither a new game nor one reserved for tabloids. Early in the 1988 contest, then vice president Bush said the anniversary of Pearl Harbor was September 7, not December 7, that evening's ABC, CBS, and NBC newscasts treated his slip like a seismic news event. Later on, when Democratic candidate Michael Dukakis's bus had a flat tire, it too was seen as a metaphor. The media billboards mistakes in part because we play a sometimes mindless game of Gotcha!, in part because we thirst for metaphors, in part because mistakes allow reporters to peel away the artificial mask candidates often hide behind.

This said, the debate among the Democratic candidates in New Hampshire was often elevated, and at least in this respect voters were more than spectators. Reporters often did spectacular work in profiling the candidates and the issues. Even when the media asked horserace or scandal-tinged questions, it was startling to watch voters sound like policy wonks when afforded a chance to ask their questions.

Still, a month before the February 18 New Hampshire primary, the "boys on the bus" were restless. They had heard the set speeches of the candidates so many times that they no longer took notes, no longer laughed at the jokes or tingled at the finale. Innocent curiosity was gone, replaced by the cynic. By January 1992, reporters were experts. They could draw thumbnail sketches of their candidates' boyhood or position on Namibia. The entire focus of their inbred lives was the candidate. From early morning to late night, they were sequestered as if in a witness protection program, moving from hotel to chartered bus or plane to rally to bus to plane to rally. They had little time to talk to voters, or shop in a supermarket, or watch television. Their transit and food and lodging were arranged, their sources were nearby, deadlines always loomed, and days and speeches blurred.

To them, news was what was *new*, and from the candidates they heard little that qualified as new. "The news media, given its norms (what's new) and imperatives (make it snappy), feel they have already covered what many voters, belatedly awakened, now want to know about," concluded the "Nine Sundays" proposal of the Barone Center at Harvard. "Since they are in the news business, the campaign press corps focuses on what is new; the new ads, the new attacks, the new polls, the new marketing techniques, the most recent article which has stirred controversy . . ." Under the pressure of constant deadlines to come up with something fresh, and constant worries about getting beat, and too little time to reflect, and with cellular telephones permitting reporters to reach the office immediately and to file stories instantly, the great enemy of thought—the sometimes mindless rush to get something *new*—always lurked.

Something new finally happened on January 23. That's the day the national *Star*, a racy supermarket tabloid, paid an undetermined sum of cash for a story that provoked a political hurricane. The story quoted Gennifer Flowers, an Arkansas state employee and sometime cabaret singer, who claimed she had carried on a twelve-year affair with Bill Clinton. Although Flowers had a year earlier denied the allegation and even threatened to sue a Little Rock radio station if it broadcast the story, the *Star* said it had tapes of conversations between Clinton and Flowers.

Clinton was confronted by the same type of media frenzy that drove Gary Hart from the race in 1987. With one big difference: The press did not do its own reporting but simply passed along rumors. At first, said Gwen Ifill, who covers Clinton for the *New York Times*, "I thought it was a tabloid story. Yet when we arrived in Nassau for a candidates' forum, there were a hundred reporters there. There was an amazing frenzy." Clinton was ambushed by reporters—Did you? Ever? Are you denying it? Instead of sticking to his own September formula that he would not stoop to answer questions that violated his "zone of privacy," the ever eager-to-persuade candidate went on and on about "checkbook journalism" and "lies" and Republican "dirty tricks." Ifill remembers how she and the other reporters on the bus "compared notes" that Thursday, wondering whether it was a legitimate story. "We had done no independent reporting," said Ifill, assuming this sensible journalistic test was adequate. Reporters knew it was all hearsay and rumor, spread by a sheet that was a newspaper in name only. Even if it were true that Clinton had had an affair with Flowers, as many reporters suspected, since Clinton was not pretending his had been a perfect marriage, why was it important?

For the first three days, or from Thursday through Sunday morning, most traditional news outlets, to their credit, resisted the story. In effect, they were telling the public: Eat your spinach! Torn between sensationalism and censorship, much of the press, what *Rolling Stone* media critic Jonathan Katz calls the major "old news" media—including the *New York Times*, the *Wall Street Journal*, the *Washington Post*, the *Los Angeles Times*, the *Chicago Tribune*, CBS, NBC, ABC, and CNN—strove to treat the story as unworthy of more than a cursory mention.

But the story attracted such a "critical mass" of reporters, observed Jack Germond, "that it became a spectacle that you could no more ignore than a huge purple elephant standing in a room." The elephant was produced by the Outsider Gang, what Katz labels the counterelite "new news" media—local TV newscasts, radio and cable call-in shows, newspaper tabloids, and tabloid TV shows like "A Current Affair" and "Hard Copy." It was hard to ignore the story because wherever Clinton went a hive of reporters followed, buzzing about with Gennifer Flowers questions. Flowers was splashed across the front pages of most tabloid newspapers. Even as she was shunted aside by the networks, she was featured on most local network-affiliated newscasts. An estimated twenty-one million viewers watched her sing "Stand by Your Man" on "A Current Affair," where the reporter thought to ask: "On a scale of one to ten, how was Clinton as a lover?" One of the most momentous events of the campaign had transpired, and the established press, properly, struggled to ignore it.

The tabloids were now in the saddle. They not only muddied the line between what was public or private behavior, between the important and the titillating, they also helped blur the distinction between the respectable and the salacious news media. It was hard not to get confused. Programs like "Hard Copy" or Geraldo Rivera's talk show did, after all, appear on network-owned stations. And sex and prurient stories were not restricted to TV tabloid shows. Diane Sawyer did ask Marla Maples on ABC, "Was it the best sex you ever had?" Tony book publishers vied for the latest celebrity tome. Because it aroused interest, hearsay was employed by *People* magazine to peek into, say, the marriage of Princess Di and Prince Charles. Docudramas now appear regularly on television, mixing fact and fiction. Director Oliver Stone, an unremitting foe of right-wing McCarthyism, nevertheless made for Warner Brothers a movie, *JFK*, in which he not only invented dialogue but had the words come from the mouths of people with real names who were sometimes portrayed as real murderers. With glee, the editor of the *Star* noted that both the *Times* and NBC News had crossed a line he would not in naming William Kennedy Smith's alleged rape victim. This was the relative defense—Everyone's doing it!

Everyone wasn't doing it, but in the public's mind the press was guilty. Surveys showed the public thought the media trivialized issues—82 percent of those polled by *Time* thought the press paid "too much" attention to the personal life of candidates. While the public was fascinated by the peephole, it was also repelled by it.

An almost panicky competitive desire to attract an audience was loose, infecting even the most serious journalists. The editors of *Time* and *Newsweek* both splashed Woody Allen on their covers in late August, perhaps confusing what was "hot" with what was important. That's the point pressed by Clinton's media adviser, Mandy Grunwald, on "Nightline" the evening the Flowers story broke. Having lost Clinton as a guest on Thursday night, Ted Koppel invited Grunwald and two others to discuss the media frenzy. "Programs like this are not a help, Ted," remonstrated Grunwald, mentioning that this was the first "Nightline" Koppel had devoted to the presidential contest. "You're telling people something that you think is important that's not in context. You're setting the agenda. And you're letting the *Star* set it for you."

Three days later, the Clintons made a fateful decision to appear on "60 Minutes" and answer questions about Flowers and their marriage. After a shrewd preemptive strike to defang the rumors at the September Sperling press breakfast, where he candidly acknowledged turbulence in their marriage but warned he would say no more about their personal life, Clinton now opened himself to queries.

The Clintons' appearance on "60 Minutes" licensed reporters to treat the Gennifer Flowers press conference the next day as a momentous event. "A decision was made months ago [by the *New York Times*] not to be the first to run a story" about Clinton's marriage, said Gwen Ifill. "After '60 Minutes,' the dam broke and we had to cover it." Hundreds of reporters packed a room at the Waldorf Astoria to inspect the bleached blond in the fire-engine red jacket who sat beside her attorney and the editor of the *Star*, just beneath a large poster reproduction of the *Star's* front page: "My 12-year Affair with Bill Clinton." Those who watched this event live on CNN, or large chunks of it as it led that evening's newscasts on all three networks, had their stereotypes of reporters comically confirmed. They heard Dick Kaplan, editor of the *Star*, suddenly transformed into Mr. Responsibility—"Please, please, please!"—as he tried to calm the hive of photographers pushing forward to get a better shot. They heard the question from an associate of the "Howard Stern Show," who wanted to know: "Did Governor Clinton use a condom?"

Minutes later came this: "Gennifer, have you slept with any other presidential candidates?"

January 27 was a Can-You-Believe-This! news day—the front page of the next day's *New York Times* screamed of Macy's filing for bankruptcy, of the Supreme Court's ruling limiting the scope of the 1965 Voting Rights Act, and of the strange disappearance of Russian president Boris N. Yeltsin. Yet the hot news this day was the lady in red. "January 27 ought to be a black day in American journalism," declared Paul Begala of the Clinton campaign. "They ought to fly the flag at half-staff at all journalism schools." Added Clinton's communications director, George Stephanopoulos: "We saw a new dynamic this campaign in which trash-for-cash tabloids dictated the news. . . . The back-door justification on the part of the press is pernicious—'it's out there and it affects the polls!'"

But it was out there, and it did impact Clinton's standing in the polls. Clinton did, stupidly, violate his own stricture not to discuss his marriage. Flowers had been placed on the state payroll, she did have tape-recorded late-night conversations with Clinton that suggested a certain intimacy, and Clinton did acknowledge it was his voice when he later apologized to Governor Cuomo for something he had said on the tapes.

Nevertheless, despite the seminars and critiques of sensationalist and brain-dead press coverage of prior campaigns, despite the media's desire to focus on issues, ABC executive producer Paul Friedman admitted, "With the best of intentions, we got swept up." An astonishing 46 percent of the more than four hundred journalists surveyed by the *Times-Mirror* poll in May 1992 concluded that questions about Clinton's character was the most important event of the contest; 20 percent said Gennifer Flowers's press conference was the most significant event of the entire campaign.

In February, the press was at the peak of its power. The Gennifer Flowers story overwhelmed the campaign. Fresh questions about Clinton's credibility were raised by a series of revelations about how he had avoided the draft in 1969. With machine-gun speed, Clinton was peppered with questions about whether he got into an ROTC program to serve or to duck the draft, whether he finally placed his name in the draft pool in order to do his duty or because he knew he was unlikely to be called, whether a letter he wrote back then opposing the Vietnam War was an eloquent expression of conscience or the work of a political weasel.

A media mindset formed about "Slick Willie," just as one had formed about "clumsy" Jerry Ford in 1976, or Bush-the-wimp in 1988. The stories almost wrote themselves. When it came to Clinton, he must be guilty of a cover-up. "One of the frustrating things about this whole deal," Clinton would later tell Garry Wills, "this nationwide attempt to make me look slick—to which I may have contributed—is that people expect me to remember things I don't remember all of, or to share things I thought I was never supposed to share."

After New Hampshire, candidates dropped any pretense at politeness and began attacking each other, knowing that the media's bias for conflict would favor them with coverage. The public correctly sensed they were mere spectators in this insider contest between candidates and the press. News was not what was vital but what was sharp. And so before this campaign would end, the Bush team would savage Democrats as godless supporters of homosexuality and Hillary Clinton as a heathen who supported the right of children to sue their parents if dissatisfied with their allowance. Not to be outdone, through the summer Clinton's team pummeled Republicans as crypto-Nazis and boasted that their team was comprised of folks like James Carville who were every bit as mad-dog mean and cynical as Lee Atwater or James Baker. Little wonder that the Barone Center report "Campaign Lessons for '92" had sadly concluded: "Elections, the litmus tests of democracy, are becoming mud-wrestling contests that are irrelevant to the realities that face the candidates once elected."

Because the contest seemed to be between the political and the media elites, citizens came to feel left out, to feel their political system was being hijacked. This is one reason so many voters protested by staying home; through the first eighteen primaries, only 30 percent of those eligible actually bothered to go to the polls.

Which brings us to Act Two of the 1992 campaign: post-Perot. The date citizens first froze the attention of the press and the candidates was February 20, 1992, the night H. Ross Perot appeared on CNN's "Larry King Live" viewer call-in show. Asked if there were "any scenario in which you would run for president" Perot responded that he might—if citizens in each of the fifty states organized and "on your own" got his name on the ballot.

Perot was treating citizens as participants, not spectators, much as FDR did with his fireside radio chats in the 1930s. Perot told King he wished "that everybody in this country would start acting like an owner," and rise up and say, "'We run this place, you guys. Listen to us.'" Perot was recognizing the power of technology to eliminate the press or party middleman. By using satellites, he could stay home and talk to voters all over America, bypassing the networks and the "boys on the bus." He could take some of the frantic quality out of a campaign, the hopscotching from airport to airport, the mindless photo ops. One day, Perot knew, citizens would be able to vote at home. One day soon they could have what he called an "electronic town hall." If he were elected president, Perot said, the first thing he would do would be to create a direct democracy through electronic town halls.

In the rush of excitement over his scoop, Larry King did not ask how such a direct democracy squared with the concept of representative government embedded in our Constitution. Wasn't our system of "checks and balances" intended to allow elected officials or appointed judges to sometimes resist the momentary demands of the mob? Wasn't it meant to frustrate the accretion of power in any one branch of government? Wasn't the Bill of Rights designed to protect individual rights from any plebiscite? King did not ask whether, if there were no press filter, candidates might not misstate facts to voters and get away with it, as happened when David Duke appeared on King's show while running for governor of Louisiana and falsely claimed he possessed letters from huge corporations eager to relocate to Louisiana if he were elected. King did not ask whether such an electronic town hall would actually make our sound-bite politics worse, eradicating all ambiguity by reducing complicated policy questions to simple yes-or-no responses. He did not ask whether the combination of money and technology might produce more Robo-candidates. Larry King is an often superb interviewer, but he's the first to say he's unburdened by detail; he takes pride in not having read books prior to chatting with authors or not having prepped beforehand so that conversations can be spontaneous.

No matter the tidal wave of support generated by Perot's February appearance on "Larry King Live," and even though the second act had begun, Act One was still not over. As primaries multiplied in March, the traditional press bias for horserace coverage, particularly on television, reasserted itself, allowing the media to play a powerful filter role. "Since New Hampshire, half of all [TV] campaign stories have focused on the horserace, more than double the coverage given to policy issues," reported the March issue of *Media Monitor*, which is produced by the Center for Media and Public Affairs in Washington. Inevitably, the level of attacks escalated, as candidates tried to trip the lead horse.

And, just as inevitably, candidates groused about the media's dual role as race caller and judge. "You folks amaze me," Clinton told CNN on the March night he triumphed in the Georgia primary. When Tsongas won the New Hampshire primary by 4 percentage points, even though he was from a neighboring state, it was reported that he won a solid "victory," said Clinton. Yet when I win Georgia, the media says it was expected because "I'm a regional candidate. . . . You act like every Southern state is just like every other one." To a pack of reporters braying about the latest polls in Dallas on March 5, Clinton refused to play the horserace game, saying, "I'm back on the issues, folks. I don't care about your political handicapping."

But reporters didn't always want to get back on the candidates' issues. Believing they were searching for clues to character, reporters continued to intrude with personal questions. ABC's Sam Donaldson put on his sheriff's badge during a March 2 interview with Bob Kerrey on "This Week with David Brinkley." There were lots of rumors about all the candidates and their personal lives, began Donaldson, who was in Washington while Kerrey appeared on a split screen from Colorado. So let's not pussyfoot:

"Did you ever use drugs?"

"No," responded Kerrey.

"Ever use marijuana?"

"No."

"Ever use cocaine?"

"No."

Donaldson thanked Kerrey for his "candid" responses, yet this viewer wished Kerrey had huffed: *None of your business, Sam! You're just fishing for a headline. You have no information, only hearsay. You haven't reported anything. Where are your sources? You're like Joe McCarthy waving an alleged list of subversives. Asking me whether I have ever used drugs is like Senator McCarthy asking: Are you now or were you ever a Communist? The insinuation leaves a stain, remaining long after the denial.*

Had Kerrey refused to answer Donaldson's query, no doubt the insects would have descended, buzzing about what he was hiding. Gotcha! may be a game, but it's one a candidate can't win. Either they get hurt for candor, or hurt for covering up.

Sometimes the rumors are less visible but just as insidious. One March morning in Houston, for example, when reporters assembled to get on the plane in the wee hours, a handful of scribes traded the latest gossip. One Washington scribe, who appears on the TV talk circuit because he gives good sound bites, knowingly whispered that Clinton was about to be hit with a knockout punch. Three potential Clinton "scandals," he said, were at that moment being investigated by the press— the *Los Angeles Times* was looking into drugs in Arkansas; a Dallas paper was chasing a woman in Dallas who supposedly had an affair with Clinton; and the *New York Times* would soon break a story about a Clinton land deal in Arkansas. In addition, he had a good source in the Bush White House who reported they were "salivating" over this turn of events, yet hoping the stories might be delayed until after Clinton was the all but certain nominee.

Not wanting to seem less than all-knowing or surprised, reporters gossiped about it. The mist of rumor would thicken as it rolled from scribe to scribe, picking up dirt. Was this the knockout blow? That afternoon, a reporter for *Newsday* asked: "What were those three stories?" He had to inform his editor so that his paper could either launch its own investigation or at least protect itself from the element of surprise.

The fear of scandal haunted both the candidate and his press entourage. The rules had fundamentally changed. Not only was it now reasonable to peer into a candidate's private life, it was also okay to print rumors. Or as George Stephanopoulos told Sidney Blumenthal for *Vanity Fair*, "It's not enough to dispute the rumor—you have to *disprove* it. The burden of proof is shifted to us, even though the accusers have zero credibility. We're guilty by suspicion, guilty until proven innocent." Clinton didn't want to get knocked out of the race by a stigma, and reporters didn't want to get beat. During March, the *Los Angeles Times* bellowed an account of a Clinton backer and state contractor who was being investigated on cocaine charges; the *New York Times* overplayed a story on Hillary and Bill Clinton's real estate dealings with a failed savings and loan banker. Each story proved not be the dreaded knockout punch.

Then came the April 7 New York primary. No Coney Island freak show can match the horrors of a New York media contest. Nowhere else in the country is the media so large and dominant. In New York City, for example, there are six powerful TV stations, four dailies, a daily Spanish-language paper, two weekly black newspapers, the weekly *New York* magazine and *Village Voice*, not to mention scores of cable and community newspapers, two all-news radio stations, and platoons of opinionated columnists who enjoy star platforms. In place of the single daily news cycle common elsewhere, in New York the news cycle never rests. Competition means a constant media game of Can-You-Top-This!

"This is New York," *New York Post* editor Jerry Nachman boasted to Howard Kurtz of the *Washington Post*. "Everything else is an out-of-town tryout." With the same sneering tough-guy swagger, Mike McAlary of the *New York Post* dismissed Hillary Clinton as "ambitious to the point of psychosis," and in print urged colleagues to mug her husband and to ask if he had ever used drugs. Local TV treated the contest like either an hourly horserace, or a Gong Show. The same night WABC-TV reported that 62 percent of New Yorkers felt the campaign was not grappling with real issues, the same local station featured stories about Clinton's electability, his wife's views on marijuana, and Governor Cuomo's role in the campaign. All stories, noted John Tierney in the *Times*, that "might have suggested a reason for [voter] discontent."

"I'm afraid that whatever I say will be subjected to one of your magical interpretations," Clinton told a press conference on April 4. When an Act Up gay-rights activist interrupted a Clinton speech, the incident was magnified because it offered the drama of conflict. Clinton came off as if he had blown his cool—much as President Bush did in July when he told POW protesters to please sit down and shut up—when in fact both Clinton and Bush politely but firmly advanced the principle of civility. Marcia Kramer of WCBS-TV made headlines when she cleverly asked Clinton whether he had smoked marijuana when a student at Oxford. Clinton dumbly answered, not only saying that he had tried it once but hastening to add that he hated it and never inhaled. The answer fit the "Slick Willie" tag affixed to Clinton.

Lost in the hysteria this answer provoked was this: the query was as mindless as the one Sam Donaldson posed to Bob Kerrey. Did the reporter have hard information? Was the information relevant? If the reason to ask was that Clinton had power, then why not ask if the president of CBS News or the editor of the *Times* also smoked the weed? And why ask it on live TV, where you are not allowed room to provide a context and where an affirmative answer implies guilt?

It was the same media mindlessness that prompted *USA Today* to think they had a scoop when they learned in April that former tennis star Arthur Ashe had AIDS. It was the same mindlessness that whipped up a local and national press frenzy about a House banking "scandal" in March, even though no public funds were stolen; by mid-April when the House released the actual list of members of Congress who overdrew their accounts, the press had flitted on to other things and this story died. It was the same mindless conformity one witnesses every time a Clinton or Bush handler stops to chat with a couple of reporters and within seconds a hive surrounds them, panicked that they are missing some vital spin from the candidate. Once after a Clinton-Brown debate in New York, Dan Balz of the *Washington Post* played for a colleague in the NBC lobby a tape of what Clinton had said to reporters that morning about how he had avoided the military draft. Although they had no idea what Balz was playing and could barely hear it, a hive soon formed and aimed their tape recorders at Balz without knowing what it was they were recording.

"Tabloid journalism is creating tabloid politics," Jesse Jackson told the *Times*. Jackson overstated it—tabloid politics is hardly new. But surely the New York contest was unusually personal and vicious. And vacuous. The same day the *Times* led its front page with a story about how federal deficits were growing and hope for future budget surpluses had dimmed, the candidates vied to ignore this reality. They kept talking, vaguely, about their promises to both increase spending and curb the deficit. They would pare "administrative costs" by at least 3 percent and tap the "peace dividend" that came from the end of the cold war. Of course, this was a form of "tabloid politics." Instead of talking about real budget cuts, or real tax increases on the nonrich, or real sacrifices

Americans (whose Social Security and Medicare and other entitlements consume half the budget) would have to make, both Clinton and Brown (like Bush) conducted misleading campaigns.

"What people don't realize is that most if not all of the 'peace dividend' is already spoken for," Congressional Budget Office Director Robert D. Reischauer told me in April 1992." Policymakers who want to protect nondefense discretionary spending from cuts over the next five years will have to devote the 'peace dividend' to meeting the spending limits in the budget agreement of 1990. So in order to increase domestic spending we either have to raise taxes a lot, or dramatically reduce spending. And there's no way to get significant new monies from taxes or spending without tapping powerful middle-class constituencies."

Rather than talk about this fiscal reality, the same day the *Times* led with its widening deficit story, Jerry Brown also landed on page one by calling Clinton a hypocrite and "Slick Willie." This outburst dominated local TV. By April 1, Clinton complained to talk-show host Phil Donahue that he and the rest of the Press Gang were just interested in "cheap thrills to make the news story of the day."

It was on this "Donahue" show that something significant happened. Looking back, if the first major assault on the press as political filter was Perot's February 20 appearance on "Larry King," the turning point in the battle may have come on the April 1 "Donahue" show. This was the moment, as Kathleen Hall Jamieson wrote, when the public seemed to seize control of the campaign from the media. Throughout the remainder of the campaign, they would compete with the press, sometimes successfully, sometimes not, to retain this power.

For the first half hour, Donahue prowled the stage with a microphone, asking Clinton: Have you ever had an affair? Have you and Hillary ever separated? A stern Clinton shot back: "We're going to sit here a long time in silence, Phil. I'm not going to answer any more of these questions." The audience lustily applauded.

Then a sheepish Donahue had his microphone gently taken by a female member of the audience, who exclaimed, "Given the pathetic state of most of the United States at this point—Medicare, education, everything else—I can't believe you spent half an hour of airtime attacking this man's character. I'm not even a Bill Clinton supporter, but I think this is ridiculous!"

Donahue was humbled by a ferocious burst of applause. He was smart and gracious enough to surrender. So Donahue let his audience submit questions, none of which concerned Clinton's marriage. This was a signal event, said John Sasso, who was Democratic nominee Michael Dukakis's principal strategist in 1988. Unlike Dukakis, who kept answering media horserace questions about how far behind he was in the polls, said Sasso, "Clinton was smart not to get sucked in" on the "Donahue" show.

Clinton was trying to manage the news, just as Nixon and Reagan and every president who contrives a White House Rose Garden strategy has done. In this case, it was hard to blame him. "We've been less accessible to the pack in New York than elsewhere," admitted Dee Dee Myers, Clinton's press secretary. This was the only hope he had "to control his message," she added.

The Donahue and King shows were not the first time the candidates bypassed the established press. Circumventing the White House press corps, in January Bush conducted a live satellite interview with a local New Hampshire TV station; honored to have a national candidate for an exclusive, local anchors tend to ask grateful questions. Brown circumvented traditional givers by devising a toll-free 800 telephone number. In New York, to prove he was a human being with a sense of humor, Clinton phoned the zany and wildly popular Don Imus radio talk show one morning. To display their policy and personal side, both Clinton and Brown separately joined Charlie Rose for provocative hour-long interviews on WNET-TV, the public TV station. The day before the New York primary, Phil Donahue won deserved kudos by inviting Clinton and Brown to sit alone at a table and just talk, without intrusion from the host or his audience (resulting in perhaps the most inspired policy discussion among candidates of the entire campaign).

By winning New York's primary on April 7, Clinton—unlike Gary Hart, who was forced to capitulate—exposed the weakness of the media. By surviving, Clinton was perceived as triumphing not only over Brown but over the media. The diminution of the "old media" bosses, wrote Richard Harwood in the *Washington Post*, "gets journalists off the stage and back into the audience where they belong." The entire establishment media structure "is coming unglued," wrote *Newsweek* media critic Jonathan Alter in the *Washington Monthly*. "We are witnessing the dawning of a new media order."

Maybe. The candidate who played that new order like a violin was H. Ross Perot. Throughout the spring, Perot seemed to be everywhere, starting with a second appearance in mid-April on "Larry King." Perot's candidacy gained credibility because he threatened to spend $100 million of his own money to promote it. To voters, Perot was more than just a rich man purchasing an office. His own informational 800 number logged more than two million calls.

Through Perot, the other candidates gleaned a better appreciation of how political communications had become decentralized. They became more aggressive. Clinton wore bebop sunglasses and played his saxophone on the "Arsenio Hall Show," fielded questions from young viewers on MTV's "Choose or Lose" program, and, demonstrating that he was not averse to baring his private life if it helped, Bill and Hillary even posed for the cover of *People* magazine in July. The morning network shows gave over one or two hours for live call-ins between voters and Clinton or Perot, which actually enlarged the regular viewing audience. Although Bush pointedly said it was unpresidential to appear on MTV or the "Donahue" show, he did belatedly consent to an interview with Barbara Walters on ABC's "20/20," to CBS's "This Morning," and to CNN and public television's "MacNeil/Lehrer NewsHour"; Vice President Dan Quayle sat for an hour with Charlie Rose. Quayle also appeared on the daily Rush Limbaugh national call-in radio show, which reaches nearly twelve million listeners on five hundred stations each week. With C-SPAN, voters could bypass the press filter and watch the actual speeches and public appearances of the candidates. By the end of July, the usually accessible Clinton went a full three weeks without a press conference or even talking to the "boys on the bus."

The candidates were declaring their independence from the press as filter, giving voice to the rage of voters, trying to give voters a sense of participation in an election.

The media were getting the message. By June, ABC executive producer Paul Friedman told the weekly *Variety*, "I don't know why, but we really missed the amount of frustration and anger out there." Friedman scheduled a week-long series of reports on voter alienation. Erik Sorenson, executive producer of "CBS Evening News," announced in early July that except in special circumstances, all quotes from candidates must be at least thirty seconds. This would allow CBS to meet "what seems to be a real yearning for information" from the voters, and would get away from the "contrived" sound bites of candidates. (In reality, as Richard L. Berke of the *Times* reported, this resulted in fewer words from the candidates, as CBS found the actual sound bites too long and unwieldy.) All three network morning news programs turned over unprecedented time to the candidates so they could field viewer questions. By the first week of July, NBC News was running two-minute snippets of the candidates' speeches, a policy soon adopted by CBS. It was meant, explained anchor Connie Chung, sitting in for Dan Rather, to give viewers an "unfiltered sense" of the candidates.

When candidates did go through a press filter, even when making fools of themselves, it didn't seem to hurt, at least initially. Perot appeared on NBC's "Meet the Press" in May, and instead of the general questions he received from Larry King, moderator Timothy J. Russert pressed him to explain exactly how he would balance the federal budget, as he had vaguely promised to do. To anyone who thought about government and policy, Perot sounded uninformed, sounded as if he were seeking a media scapegoat when he accused Russert and the other reporters of trying to ambush him. Yet soon after this appearance, Perot announced that he intended to curtail his public appearances and interviews with newspapers and newsmagazines. He would have nothing further to say about policy for at least sixty days, or until he had consulted "experts." Still, Perot continued to zoom in the polls. By early June, after Bush and Clinton had locked up their party nominations, Perot actually pulled ahead of them in head-to-head voter surveys. "Any time there's confrontation, the phone circuits blow away," Perot told Elizabeth Drew of the *New Yorker*.

The Perot technique of bypassing reporters was taken a step further in California, where candidates were bypassing voters as well. Congressman Mel Levine, who sought the Democratic Senate nod, shunned the normal bumper stickers and buttons and shook few hands as he made only about twelve public appearances between March and the June 2 primary. Instead Levine spent his days "dialing for dollars," with the $5 million he collected earmarked for TV ads. As Levine explained to Jane Gross of the *New York Times*, "talking to people is just spinning our wheels."

Levine's opponents charged that he was trying to buy the election, a charge not novel in an election year. What was novel was the technology, which permitted candidates to campaign differently. "If candidates' ability to shape news coverage was the news of 1988," concluded Kathleen Hall Jamieson, "the news of 1992 is the ability of candidates to bypass news entirely. The reason: the rise of talk radio and television."

◆ ◆ ◆

What the 1992 contest demonstrates is that we are in a transition period between Acts Two and Three. But transition to what? Candidates and citizens alike had every reason to be irate about the insectlike behavior of the press. But without the filter of either a party or a vigilant press corps, there's a real danger candidates could snooker voters. Or they could pretend, as Perot did, that the elixir for our woes was more direct democracy when, in fact, it could be argued candidates already listened too intently to voters. After all, it is for fear of offending voters that public officials won't curb mushrooming entitlement spending, or narrow the federal deficit, or impose gun control, or legislate stricter energy conservation standards, including a gasoline tax to curb America's dangerous dependency on foreign oil and to help cleanse the environment.

Technology is neutral; it is not the enemy. The true enemies are thoughtless candidates, thoughtless reporters, and thoughtless citizens. Technology will permit future candidates to bypass the press more skillfully. But it is by no means certain this Brave New World has arrived. After all, media criticism of Mel Levine's arrogant campaign helped defeat him in California. More telling, a series of tough and thorough exposés of Perot's business and personal dealings, particularly in the *New York Times*, no doubt contributed to his stunning mid-July withdrawal from the race.

The "boys on the bus" still framed much of the summer's political news. President Bush in late July and August would suffer from the media mindset that he was a loser—as Bill Clinton had in June when press insiders were convinced he could never overcome the "character issue" and were persuaded that Perot's presence in the race devastated the Democrat. Then, as happened to Clinton in January, a tabloid headline (in this case, in the *New York Post*) unleashed a new insect attack.

The August front-page headline was triggered by a thirty one-line footnote in a new book, *The Power House*, by Susan B. Trento. The footnote leans on an interview (by someone else) with a former American arms-control negotiator (now dead) who shared his (non-tape-recorded) impression that Vice President Bush had a 1984 tryst in Geneva (the source admitted he couldn't be sure). The author also couldn't be sure, which is why she buried this footnote on page 413.

The *Post* seized on the footnote as a welcome excuse to be first in print with a decade-old rumor based on no direct witnesses or facts, only hearsay. Surprisingly, the resulting frenzy was tripped by an established press institution, CNN, in the person of White House reporter Mary Tillotson. Although she did no independent sleuthing, Tillotson nevertheless startled Bush at a press conference by asking about the *Post* headline. Bush called the question "sleazy."

When Tillotson was telephoned later to be asked why a serious journalist (she is) would heave such a live grenade, this lion of the Fourth Estate meekly had her calls intercepted by a CNN spokesman, who said, "Mary's not doing interviews."

The insects were loose. That afternoon on radio and television, analysts discussed the impact of the rumors on the race. And then that night Stone Phillips happened to have an NBC interview with Bush. Without expending any more effort than Tillotson or the *Post*, Phillips asked the president: "Have you ever had an affair?"

With firmness, Bush responded, "You're perpetuating the sleaze by even asking the question."

Phillips coolly defended himself, insisting the question "goes to the point of character." Bush didn't call Phillips a scoundrel, but he did say, "I should think you'd be ashamed of yourself."

It wasn't possible to learn if Phillips was ashamed, because he prefers to ask questions, not answer them. But an NBC spokeswoman, Tory Beilinson, did say it was a "double standard" for Bush to promote "family values and then say it is 'sleazy' when you are asked about one of those values, which is marital fidelity."

Of course, Phillips was sleazy to perpetuate rumors. Moreover, assume that "marital fidelity" were a "family value." Is it a value central to being a good president? Should we not have elected Thomas Jefferson or FDR? Don't reporters have an obligation to do some homework before hurling damaging questions in public? And if reporters have license to buzz around the issue of "marital fidelity," should we also seek proof that the public couple actually sleep together? Is their relationship genuine? What if a public figure received mental solace, but not sex, from a dalliance?

Not surprisingly, as Clinton supporters did in their winter of discontent, Republicans now aimed their cannons at the media for foisting "sleaze" upon the American people. Reporters insisted that once the story was out and the president of the United States was asked about it publicly, they couldn't ignore the story. True. But in this case, as in so many others throughout the 1992 campaign, we see why reporters are viewed as insects.

So how'd the press do in 1992? "Campaign coverage is better, and worse this year," aptly summarizes David Marannis of the *Washington Post.* Through Labor Day, the press could boast of having paid more attention to substance and to monitoring the TV ads of the candidates; television chased fewer staged photo opportunities; there was, said Republican Roger Ailes before Bush's miserable summer, "more even-handed coverage—they are picking on Democrats as well as Republicans." Another plus this year was that the public received more unfiltered information from more sources than ever before. "I think it will continue in the general election," predicted David Broder. "That's an improvement over 1988 and 1984, when the only thing the public saw from the winning candidate was what the candidate chose to put on the air themselves." Never again, thinks Broder, will the press—or the candidate—be the sole traffic cop, filtering information for voters.

Of course, as Broder shared his thoughts in the lobby of New York's Intercontinental Hotel during July's Democratic convention, candidate Bill Clinton entered the lobby and was immediately ambushed by shouted questions. That morning, as Clinton left the hotel, abortion protesters tried to hand him a dead fetus. "Governor, what did you think of that fetus this morning?" shouted reporters, looking for a sharp sound bite.

In a way, this scene captures the essential weakness of the press pack, and not just the weaknesses of the Outsider Gang. As smart and as much fun as the "boys on the bus" are, the culture of the press—Is it new? Is it sharp? Is it a good picture or bite?—often wars with the complex nature of reality. We offer saturation coverage, say, of the Los Angeles riots in May, but not sustained year-round coverage of inner cities. What coverage we get tends to squeeze reality into a left-right continuum—either racism or the breakdown of order is the villain; either bad social conditions or bad people are the cause of crime. Never both. Liberals blame government, conservatives blame bad values. In truth, sometimes both are, simultaneously, true. Yet too often this gray truth does not fit into the "Crossfire" or "McLaughlin & Co." format with its either/or choices, or into simple headlines or ninety-second TV pieces.

The process can be mindless. Although we reporters like to think of ourselves as individualists, the process also demonstrates conformity. We vie to shout questions in a pack. We seek sound bites, not always information. We abhor the tabloids which break stories about Clinton's or Bush's alleged affairs, yet we blah, blah, blah about the political impact of these developments on the contest. We simplify and shy from ambiguity. We too rarely report on each other. We adopt the all-knowing posture, which creates the conventional wisdom that has been so wrong this year—from Bush is a shoo-in (September 1991) to Cuomo is the one (November) to no third-party candidate stands a chance (winter) to Clinton cannot win (spring) to Bush is dead (summer). We affect a macho, tough-guy swagger. Worse than being beat on a story is to have it whispered that a scribe is in the pocket of a candidate.

As in any gang, peer pressure plays a role. When reporters David Broder and Bob Woodward went against the grain in late 1991 with a *Washington Post* series suggesting that Dan Quayle, while no rocket scientist, was no dolt either, colleagues said they had gone in the tank for Quayle. In fact, the portrait of Quayle, while rounded, could be read as devastating. While Quayle was shown to be politically shrewd and more influential than thought within White House councils, he was also shown—not asserted—to be unread, unreflective, preoccupied with playing golf, and sometimes dominated by an ideological, unforgiving wife who flashes teeth like a talk-show host but hates like Pat Buchanan.

The peer pressure to define news as new, to focus on the horserace or conflict—on what's hot—too often leads reporters away from government-oriented stories. Our political coverage is often either personality-driven, like a soap opera with an ongoing narrative, or episodic, like "the beam of a searchlight," as once described by Walter Lippmann, "that moves restlessly about, bringing one episode and then another out of darkness into vision. Men cannot do the work of the world by this light alone. They cannot govern society by episodes, incidents, and interruptions."

On this point, there seems to be little dissent. According to a May *Times-Mirror* poll of more than four hundred leading journalists, two-thirds (67 percent) believe there has been "insufficient focus on the real issues at stake in this contest." Starting with Theodore H. White's pioneering *The Making of the President* in 1960, the press has invested more effort covering the drama and personalities than the issues a president is elected to address. The dirty little secret, Ronald Reagan's media maestro, Michael Deaver, has said many times, is that the television press in particular is too often driven less by news considerations than they like to admit. They want pictures and ratings and drama and good sound bites, and time is their enemy. What "we figured out in the seventies and eighties," Deaver told David Brinkley, "is that network news was not news, it was entertainment."

Inevitably, wrote Jay Rosen of New York University in *Tikkun* magazine, campaigns are covered "like a football season: First we find out who plays in the Super Bowl, then we see who wins. . . . Who wins may be the relevant question for football fans; as citizens we need to know what wins—what the polity is deciding about itself when it selects a president. Is a vote for candidate X a vote for national health care? Is a victory by candidate Y a statement that the former Soviet Union can find its own way to democracy?. . . Let the election produce a winner; the campaign is about the production of *meaning*. Unless, of course, it is drained of meaning by those who help construct it."

Instead of asking "Who's winning? Is it new?" journalists should more often ask, "Is it important?" The media asks surface questions for many reasons, not the least being that it seems easier to maintain our "objective" neutrality by reporting who wins or loses primaries or who's ahead in the polls than by reporting who's right or wrong or what it all means. Yet if we abandon the idea of "objectivity," however illusory it may be, we skate on glass. We risk becoming partisans, or being perceived as such, which would drain the press of whatever credibility it retains.

However, the bottom line is that the press can do a better job of providing voters with what they need to make informed choices. Citizens, as Christopher Lasch has observed, need controversy and debate, not just information, to make informed choices. Information is merely a "by-product" of debate, he writes. "When we get into arguments we become avid seekers of relevant information. Otherwise we take in information passively, if we take it in at all."

No doubt, the media will learn from some of the mistakes they made in 1992, just as we learned from 1988 and earlier contests. But while we learn, so have voters and the candidates. One day history may say of this contest that it represents the final gasp of power from the "boys on the bus" and the start of something new.

That something new may be the opportunity to campaign for president in a wholly different, and perhaps dangerous, way. In the future, a candidate can bypass not just the press but his own party. If the press wants to regain its sometimes necessary role as filter, it needs to reclaim its lost credibility. To do that, it would be salutary to have the networks make more time available to the candidates, or for the networks and the "new media" to withstand commercial pressures and uphold their public trust, or for the press in general to adopt many of the recommendations that gush from foundations and scholars.

A number of reform proposals have bounced about that make sense, including:

1. The "Nine Sundays" idea advanced by the Joan Shorenstein Barone Center at Harvard, which urges the networks and

other television stations to voluntarily set aside ninety minutes on the nine Sundays between Labor Day and Election Day for debates and a serious probe of presidential issues;

2. The ceding by local stations of a half hour of local news time so the networks can expand to a nightly one-hour newscast in the fall (in exchange, the stations would retain the right to sell much of the ad time);

3. The commitment by television and radio to airing longer sound bites from the candidates; as CBS News somewhat fitfully tried this year;

4. Devoting more space to consumer reports on the truthfulness of campaign advertising; as CNN and some newspapers have pioneered;

5. Creating more peer pressure for good journalism. To do this, the print and electronic press could:(a) cover itself more aggressively; or (b) hire a press ombudsman who reports to the publisher or general manager, not to the editor or executive producer; or (c) borrow a technique used on "60 Minutes" of broadcasting letters to the editor; or (d) downplay horserace coverage by giving less space to polls and by spreading awareness that predicting winners and losers weeks before a vote is just as intrusive as a network projecting the winner before the polls even close on election night; or (e) initiate Pulitzer-like prizes for the best televised campaign coverage.

But blue-ribbon panels such as ours should not stray from some simple truths. One is that the fundamental flaw of campaign press coverage is this: mindlessness. Too often the form of journalism—gimme a headline, gimme drama, gimme pictures, gimme no more than a minute, thirty seconds—dictates the content. Even with the best intentions—and the intentions are usually noble—this flaw is commonplace. And despite notable differences between the two, it is a trait too often shared by the "new" as well as the "old" media.

Another shared trait: Unlike in most tribal societies, the element of shame is a potent and too neglected tool to check the abuse of journalistic power. It is easy for us to flick off criticism from Bush or Clinton as self-serving. Or even to proclaim that polls revealing how unpopular we are is nothing new, just a way of shooting the messenger. One way to penetrate our insularity is to encourage more sustained press criticism. Peer pressure is as potent within a press gang as within a street gang. To alter behavior we need alter the peer pressure. Journalists might regain some lost credibility if we more often rebuked miscreants by name, if we behaved less like an elite gang of fellow insiders or smart alecks and more like the champions of "the public trust" we proclaim ourselves to be.

LET THE PRESS BE THE PRESS:
PRINCIPLES OF CAMPAIGN REFORM

THOMAS E. PATTERSON

Public opinions must be organized for the press if they are to be sound, not by the press as is the case today."[1] With his usual clarity, Walter Lippmann thus stated what he believed had become a major defect in the practice of American politics. The year was 1922.

Since then, the United States has edged ever closer to a democracy that requires the press to organize its political choices. Nowhere is this more true than in the presidential selection process. Even if the news media did not want responsibility for organizing the campaign, it is theirs by virtue of an election system built upon numerous primaries, self-generated candidacies, and weak political parties.

Lippmann's argument, however, remains as valid today as when he made it years ago. When Lippmann spoke of "public opinions," he was not speaking of people's attitudes on the topical issues of the day, which is how pollsters narrowly define the term; Lippmann used the term to describe "the pictures in our heads of the world outside." Public opinions consist, he wrote, of people's "pictures of themselves, of others, of their needs, purposes, and relationship." These pictures are a pseudoworld, but it is to these pictures, not the real world, that our actions are a response. "To traverse the world men must have maps of the world," Lippmann wrote. "Their persistent difficulty is to secure maps on which their own need, or someone else's need, has not sketched in the coast of Bohemia."[2]

The news cannot provide the maps that the public requires for guidance. The function of news, as Lippmann noted, is "to signalize events" and to bring to light the unseen facts.[3] The job of setting these facts in order so that we can act upon them is the job of political leaders and institutions.

This is not to say that news organizations are somehow inferior to political institutions but rather that each has a different role and responsibility. Democratic elections cannot operate effectively without a free press acting effectively in its sphere. Yet the news media should not be asked to do the job intended for political institutions. When we ask the press to operate in their stead, it is bound to fail us, no matter how determined its effort.

The belief that the press can substitute for political institutions is widespread. Critics and apologists alike expect the press to save the campaign from its distortions, and to shape the voters' opinions. Many journalists, perhaps most of them, assume that they can do this effectively. Many scholars who study the media also accept the idea that the press can organize the election. Every four years, they suggest that the campaign would be coherent if only it were reported differently.

The marked improvement in election coverage in 1992 will help to strengthen the belief that the press can organize the campaign. Carl Bernstein has declared that this year's coverage closely approximated "the ideal of what good reporting has always been: the best obtainable version of the truth."[4] Lippmann categorically rejected such claims. "News and truth," he said, "are not the same thing, and must be clearly distinguished."[5]

If Lippmann's view is the correct one, we need to assess our expectations of the press as thoroughly as we judge its performance. We need to examine why the press cannot do the job that the modern campaign asks of it. Although this view may seem to be the most extreme form of press criticism, it relieves the news media of the assumption that they can give Americans a coherent campaign. The press has its own responsibilities. Let the press be the press, and not also a stand-in for defective political institutions.

This position leads to a different perspective on election communication than we are accustomed to taking. Rather than asking more of the press, we might ask:

1.   How might election journalism be changed to relieve the press of responsibilities it has assumed but cannot or ought not perform?

2.   How might election communication be restructured to place more of the burden of organizing election opinion and debate on political leaders and institutions?

3. How might the electoral process be restructured to reduce the undue burden that the modern campaign places on the press?

Before addressing these questions, I will discuss more fully the responsibilities that the modern campaign assigns the press, and will examine why the press cannot fulfill all of them. My arguments are taken in part from a book (titled *Out of Order*) that I am writing for Knopf.

THE PRESS'S ROLE IN THE CAMPAIGN

The news media's role in presidential campaigns changed fundamentally in the early 1970s when the political parties surrendered their hold on the nominating process. Until then party leaders had controlled nominations. The primaries gave candidates the opportunity to demonstrate popular support, but the real power of nomination rested with the party leadership. In 1952, for example, Estes Kefauver won twelve of thirteen primaries he entered, but lost his party's nomination to Adlai Stevenson, who was favored by the party leaders.

In 1968, the nomination of Hubert Humphrey, who had not entered a single primary, further divided a Democratic party already split over Vietnam. When he lost the election, the Democrats adopted reforms that shifted control of delegate selection to rank-and-file voters. The McGovern–Fraser commission mandated that a state's national-convention delegates would have to be chosen in either a primary election or in caucuses open to all rank-and-file party members who wanted to participate.

The change to a voter-centered system greatly increased the press's influence. No amount of support from party leaders could substitute for the support of millions of rank-and-file voters. A Humphrey-type campaign for nomination could no longer succeed. Any politician who seriously wanted to be considered for nomination had to campaign through the media to the people.

This reform was implemented with no apparent recognition that the responsibility for organizing the campaign had been shifted from the party to the press. The McGovern–Fraser commission's report, *Mandate for Reform*, included no systematic evaluation of the press's role in the new system. The report had a single message: rank-and-file voters would be the kingmakers in the new system.[6]

This notion, however, was based on a naive understanding of the public. The new system was plebiscitelike, but the decision it gave to voters was much too complex for them to grasp without help. The system did not pose a yes-no vote on a single issue of policy or leadership;

rather, it asked voters to make a complicated decision that even seasoned party professionals, operating in the context of a deliberative national convention, have difficulty making.

The voters would have to get help from somewhere. The real choice that the McGovern–Fraser commission faced in 1970 was not the choice between a system with the party leaders in the middle and a system with no one in the middle: in a polity of any size, a complex interaction between the public and its leaders requires an intermediary. The choice was whether the party or some other agent would act as mediator. Since the only other possible agent was the press, the McGovern–Fraser commission chose it without recognizing that it had done so.

The full significance of the change also escaped the notice of the prestige press. Not a single editorial, analysis piece, or news story about the press's role in the new system appeared in the prestige press when the McGovern–Fraser reforms were adopted.[7] The first campaign under the new system did not alter the situation. In *The Boys on the Bus*, Timothy Crouse described a campaign press corps soured by Vietnam and increasingly adversarial, but otherwise engaged in business as usual.[8]

If journalists today recognize the centrality of their role, they are not always sure of what they should do to fulfill it. The decision by the editors of *Time*, the *New Republic*, and *New York* magazine to anoint Bill Clinton by placing him on their front covers in January of 1992, before the voters had begun even to consider their choices, revealed a deep misunderstanding of what is required of the press if the voters are to exercise *their* discretion.

Such misunderstandings, however, are a secondary concern. The main problem is that the press does not have the capacity to carry out the role that the modern campaign assigns to it. The proper organization of electoral opinion requires an institution with certain characteristics. It must be able to see the world steadily. It must have the incentive to identify and bring together those interests that are making demands for policy representation. And it must be accountable for its choices, so that the public can reward it when satisfied, and force corrections upon it when dissatisfied.[9]

The press has none of these characteristics. The press has its special strengths, but they are not these strengths.

REFRACTED IMAGES OF THE CAMPAIGN

Because it lacks these characteristics, the pictures of the campaign that the press provides are not adequate to the voters' needs. If news values are not so bizarre that they produce a "map" of the election on which has been "sketched the coast of Bohemia," they do result in a highly refracted portrayal of what is at stake in the campaign. Insofar as the voters depend on the news in forming their impressions of what the election is about, they get pictures that are not balanced, but rather ones in which are embedded the values of journalism.

In this section, I will discuss two tendencies that illustrate how news values slant election coverage. These tendencies were selected in part because they can be documented adequately within the relatively small space available to me in this paper.*

Tendency 1: Good Press, Bad Press. The press's traditional political role is that of watchdog. In the campaign, this role has meant that journalists take responsibility for protecting the public against deceitful and unfit candidates. This responsibility, however, is not the same one that was imposed on the press when the nominating system was opened wide in the early 1970s. The newer responsibility requires the press to act constructively in order to create a reliable and coherent picture of the campaign upon which the voters can act.

The press's watchdog role conflicts with its newer one. Since the Progressive era, the press has viewed politicians skeptically. "The journalists' instinct," the sociologist Michael Schudson writes, "is that there is always a story *behind* the story, and that it is 'behind' because someone is hiding it."[10] For a long period, this instinct was held in check by the rules of objective journalism. Even as late as two decades ago, the journalist Carl Leubsdorf was able to say: "It is my job to report what

---

*With more space, I could have examined other tendencies, which are more complex and perhaps more intriguing. For example, the tone of election news inevitably favors some candidates over others. Studies by Harvard's Barone Center, the Washington-based Center for Media and Public Affairs, and others have shown that the tone of the coverage of George Bush during the 1992 election was measurably less favorable than that of Bill Clinton. Such evidence is often said by critics to indicate the press's partisan bias. The press defends itself from these charges by saying that its coverage reflected "reality," that there actually was more bad news to be told of one of the candidates. My own analysis suggests that a third explanation, "journalistic bias," is more accurate than either of the conventional ones. In examining the news coverage of all major-party nominees between 1960 and 1988, I have been able to identify four situationally defined "story lines" that are used by the press in the reporting of candidates. These story lines are based on news values, but they vary in the degree to which they portray a candidate unfavorably. Bush's candidacy conformed, situationally, with the least favorable of these story lines, so he received the worst press. This coverage hurt Bush's reelection effort, but the bias was journalistic rather than partisan in nature. This tendency and others will be discussed in my forthcoming book.

the candidate says, whether I believe it or not."[11] This restraint crumbled with Vietnam and Watergate, when the deceptions of the Johnson and Nixon administrations convinced reporters that they had let the nation down by taking political leaders at their word. Two presidents had lied, so no politician's words would be trusted.

Since then, election news has been as much a barrier between candidates and voters as it has been a bridge between them. Election after election the voters are told by the press that the candidates are not worthy of their support. "I know a lot of people who are thinking about this election the same way they think about the Iran-Iraq war," wrote Meg Greenfield in 1980. "They desperately want it to be over, but they don't want anyone to win." George Will said much the same thing in 1992: "The congestion of debates may keep these guys off the streets for a few days. When they emerge from the debates, November—suddenly the loveliest word in the language—will be just around the corner."[12]

These are not the isolated opinions of two critics. Studies show that candidates routinely get "bad press." The best study to date on this subject is Michael Robinson and Margaret Sheehan's *Over the Wire and on TV*, which examined CBS and UPI coverage of the 1980 election. Robinson and Sheehan excluded explicit references by journalists to a candidate's chances of winning, and focused on whether the other things said about the candidate could be considered favorable or unfavorable. If a news story had three times as much positive as negative information about the principal candidate involved, it was considered "good news." If it had three times as much negative as positive information, it was regarded as "bad news." Events in and of themselves were not regarded as good or bad; they were recorded as such only if what was concluded from them was positive or negative to the candidate.[13]

Robinson and Sheehan found that the tendency of candidates to receive "bad press" was more pronounced in some situations, more true of some candidates, and more prevalent on television, but was, nonetheless, a general pattern. Reporters, they concluded, "do seem to want to make the public aware of the frailties and inadequacies of their elected leadership."[14]

My content analysis of 1960–1988 election coverage (the 1992 component of this analysis is still in progress) measured "bad press" and "good press" in a somewhat different way than did Robinson and Sheehan's,* but it confirms their findings.[15] The studies so far of 1992 election news are also consistent with Robinson and Sheehan's findings.

---

*The primary difference in methodology was that I evaluated each news message with a scale that ran from "very favorable" to "very unfavorable." The figures cited are based on the scale, excluding messages that were evaluated as neutral. Like Robinson and Sheehan's, my analysis excludes direct references to the candidates' chances.

Bush's coverage was the least favorable, but Clinton and Perot also received a heavy dose of bad press.[16]

Most bad-press stories criticize candidates for "contradicting themselves, behaving politically or engaging in symbolism."[17] The press debunks most of the candidates' promises, implying that they either don't intend to fulfill them or couldn't keep their promises if they tried. This tendency toward skepticism was routinized this year by regular features such as MacNeil/Lehrer's "Fact or Fiction" and CBS's "Reality Check." The message of these news features was that candidates are magicians at best, liars at worst.

In fact, however, presidential candidates have a good record of keeping their promises. Political scientist Gerald Pomper's exhaustive study of party platforms found that victorious presidential candidates, once in office, try to fulfill nearly all of the planks and succeed in fulfilling most of them. When they fail to deliver on a promise, it is often because they can't get Congress to enact it.[18]

Michael Krukones reached the same conclusion after comparing the campaign speeches and in-office performances of eleven recent presidents.[19] Ian Budge and Richard I. Hofferbert echoed the conclusion in their study: they found "strong links between postwar (1948–1985) election platforms and governmental outputs."[20] I know of no study that supports the press's contention that candidates for the presidency regularly make promises they either cannot or will not fulfill.

Of course, a campaign is sometimes plagued by deceit, and the voters should be told about it. It is probably safe to say that no presidential candidate has gone through an entire campaign without once having made an intentionally misleading promise. The press, however, treats almost every campaign promise as a calculated deception. When candidates are presented in this way, the bond between the public and its leadership is weakened. There was a point in the 1992 campaign when all three of the major candidates were seen unfavorably by the public. This perception changed substantially during the debates, when the voters had the opportunity to see the candidates through something other than the lens of daily news reporting. Nevertheless, as in all recent elections, many Americans in 1992 went to the polls on Election Day believing, as they had repeatedly been told to believe, that their choice was between the "lesser of two evils."

Tendency 2: Reporters' Issues, Candidates' Issues. Election coverage was measurably better in several respects in 1992 than in past elections. There was more coverage of the issues, more stories on the candidates' backgrounds, less emphasis on the horserace, and a greater attempt to give context to daily coverage. These were not small achievements, and they will likely be sustained in future campaigns.

The question of issues, however, is not simply one of how much coverage the issues receive but of whether this coverage reflects the choices being offered the voters. In this respect, election news in 1992, as in previous years, was misshapen.

The issues that candidates stress most heavily are not those reported most heavily by the press. Candidates base their campaigns on broad policy commitments, such as promises to keep the peace and to promote prosperity, and on specific pledges to the groups and interests aligned with their party. These issues dominate the candidates' efforts because they are the issues that have the greatest impact on the voters.

These issues, however, tend not to be the favorites of reporters. The candidates' coalitional appeals are thought to be too narrow to be of general news interest, and their broad appeals are often seen as too vague for easy use. Moreover, these issues usually do not involve the conflict that reporters prefer in news stories. Gerald Pomper's research indicates that only one in ten issue pledges places the candidates in directly opposing positions. Most of the positions that candidates take either overlap with their opponents' positions or appeal to different groups of voters.[21] Finally, the candidates' basic appeals are repetitious, contained in finely tuned stump speeches that are repeated at nearly every campaign stop and before nearly every audience. "When the candidates say the same things over and over," says television correspondent Judy Woodruff, "it is not news."

Journalists like what Colin Seymour-Ure has called "clear-cut issues,"[22] those that neatly divide the candidates, are based on principle, and can be stated in simple terms, usually by reference to a shorthand label, such as "character" or "Murphy Brown."

The press's preference for clear-cut issues stems from its view of what constitutes news. James David Barber writes, "The reporter's raw material is differences—between what was and what is, expectations and events, reputations and realities, normal and exotic—and his artful eye is set to see the moment when the flow of history knocks two differences together."[23] Thus the issues that sharply identify the candidates are preferred to those on which their differences are imprecise, complex, or small.

The attention that "Oxford" and "Moscow" received in the closing month of the 1992 campaign illustrates the lure that clear-cut issues have for the press. News of Clinton's visit to the Soviet Union as a graduate student far overshadowed such October issues as Clinton's elaboration of his position on the North American Free Trade Agreement, new CIA revelations on the U.S. government's role in the arming of Iraq, and a change in Clinton's health-care proposal.[24]

When Bush questioned Clinton's trip during an interview on "Larry King Live," it exploded into the headlines in a way that policy issues seldom do. Policy issues make news for a day or two here and there around a candidate's speech or another event, but they are seldom the subject of ongoing news stories. A study found that more than 50 percent of clear-cut issues get extended news coverage (at least one story for two days running), as compared with only 15 percent of broad policy issues.[25]

Some clear-cut issues are more appropriately called "campaign issues" than "policy issues." Campaign issues are ones that arise from errors in judgment by the candidates. When campaign issues break, they make the headlines and top the television newscasts. They often trigger what Larry Sabato calls a "feeding frenzy."[26] Even a short list of such issues from recent campaigns illustrates the prominence to which they have risen: ethnic purity, the *Playboy* interview, the Eastern Europe gaffe (1976); Reagan's ethnic jokes, the debate about the debates, Vietnam as a "noble cause" (1980); Ferraro's taxes, Bush's "kicked a little ass" remark, "Hymietown" (1984); Biden's plagiarizing, Donna Rice, Dukakis's mental history (1988); Gennifer Flowers, the other Jennifer, potato with an "e" (1992).

Campaign issues have a special appeal to the press in part because they conform with traditional news values—they are unexpected, colorful, and unique. Who could have guessed that the vice president of the United States would correct a twelve-year-old boy by telling him that he had left the "e" off the word "potato"? Who would have imagined that a staunchly anticommunist president would say in 1976 that Eastern Europe was free of Soviet domination? The ongoing content analysis of the Center for Media and Public Affairs provides an indication of the media's concern with clear-cut issues during the 1992 campaign. In September, for example, policy issues (the economy led the way in this category) got a lot more attention than in most months, but they got less attention than did campaign issues. The Center reported: "The greatest media attention in September (126 stories) went to campaign trail controversies. These short-term flare-ups included disputes over Clinton's draft record, Perot's on-again, off-again candidacy, Bush's veracity on his Iran-contra role, and the Republicans' allegedly low-road campaign tactics."[27]

To be sure, candidates do not ignore such issues. When the opponent blunders or is otherwise vulnerable, candidates attack. Increasingly, too, candidates respond to attacks by their opponents with counterattacks.

In general, though, clear-cut issues are of less concern to the candidates than to the press, a conclusion supported by Benjamin Page's exhaustive study of election issues. He found that every presidential nominee, including ideologues like Barry Goldwater and George McGovern, stressed general goals and coalition appeals more than specific disputes.[28] How different are the issue agendas of journalists and candidates? A study that compared candidates' speeches with election news found an inverse emphasis on clear-cut issues. Such issues comprised only a third of the issue content of the candidates' speeches but two-thirds of the issue content of election news.[29] The critical agenda, of course, is the candidate's. The economic plan that Bill Clinton proposed in a speech at Georgetown University in early December 1991 was nearly the same as the plan described in his acceptance speech at the Democratic National Convention, and closely parallels what, by early accounts, will define the initiatives of his administration. If voters wanted to know what a Clinton presidency promised, their best guide was what candidate Clinton was saying.

DIRECTIONS FOR REFORM: JOURNALISM

The tendencies I have just described illustrate the large gap that exists between the news coverage and the reality of political choice in a presidential campaign. The challenge of reform is to move the version of the campaign that Americans see and hear through the mass media of communication closer to the political reality. This challenge can be met in part through changes in election journalism.

In his essay "News, Truth, and a Conclusion," Walter Lippmann sought to distinguish news from truth, arguing that they coincide only at those few points "where social conditions take recognizable and measurable shape."[30] All else in the news is opinion.

This distinction between "truth" and "opinion" gives us a basis for deciding which tendencies in election coverage we are content to let the press keep, and which we would ask it to avoid. The more the news reflects opinion, particularly when coupled with partisan consequences, the more it should be avoided. As election news slides into the realm of opinion and works to the disadvantage of one candidate, the other, or both, it becomes less acceptable. With this formulation in mind, I would like to suggest two things the press should not do:

1. The Press Should Not Judge Motives. One area where journalists' opinions prevail in the news is in their presumption that the candidates do not stand for anything, that they will say whatever is needed to win the election and then act as they please in office. This view, as I indicated earlier, is not supported by the evidence. Candidates tend to keep their promises.

The attribution of motives is a risky business under the best of circumstances. Often, the person engaged in a particular act cannot untangle the complex web of motives that led to it. How then can the press, looking at the candidates from the outside, know that their promises are calculated deceptions? The answer is that the press cannot know this.

The press can get away with these charges because the campaign takes place in the future tense. In this respect, the campaign situation is different from the governing situation. If reporters say an official has acted improperly in a particular instance, there can be an appeal to past or present evidence: Did he, or didn't he? The campaign is a different situation. The candidates' speeches are filled with promises of what they *will* do if elected. The answer to whether they will keep a promise is in the future, so the press is free to speculate. Who can refute the journalist's claim that the candidates have no intention of keeping their promises?

This kind of journalism wrongfully and needlessly weakens the capacity of the candidates to mobilize the electorate. News that repeatedly says the candidates' promises are deceptions fosters cynicism and mistrust on the part of the voters.

Since the 1960s, the public's support for its final two presidential-candidate choices has steadily declined. More than half the candidates in this period have had, overall, an unfavorable rating with the voters. Before the 1970s, it was rare for a major-party nominee to have a negative image with the electorate as a whole. Have presidential candidates actually grown steadily worse? A better explanation is found in the increase in negative news coverage. My content analysis of 1960–1988 coverage indicates that candidates' news coverage grew steadily worse. In 1960, about 75 percent of evaluative news messages about Kennedy and Nixon, together, were positive; by 1988, Bush and Dukakis, together, received only 43 percent positive coverage. Is it any surprise that voters have had increasingly negative opinions of presidential candidates?

I am not suggesting that the press should always take the candidates at their word; the burden of proof, however, should fall on the press rather than the candidates. If reporters can demonstrate, conclusively, that a candidate's promise cannot be reconciled with the candidate's past performance or with other major factors, the press should say so, but when a Democratic candidate goes before a traditionally Democratic group and makes a traditionally Democratic promise, it is intellectually dishonest to imply that the candidate's promise is a vote-getting ploy.

Because the burden of proof should fall on the press rather than the candidates, features such as CBS's "Reality Check" and MacNeil/Lehrer's "Fact or Fiction" are a bad idea. These features carry the presumption that candidates do not tell the truth. Armed with this presumption, the journalist can always find fault with something a candidate has said.

This type of reporting is not watchdog journalism; it is a threat to the press's watchdog role. What Alexander Hamilton said of the foundation of the judiciary's power—"it has only judgment"—applies also to the press. In the long run, the tendency of the press to cry deception at every conceivable opportunity can only weaken its capacity to make the voters take notice when a critical deception actually occurs.

2. The Press Should Not Speak for the Candidates. In earlier times, election news gave the candidates an opportunity to present themselves on their own terms to the voters. Today, journalists do most of the candidates' talking for them.

In a study that compared the *New York Times*'s coverage of the elections of 1896, 1928, 1960, and 1984, Kristi Andersen and Stuart Thorson found that the candidates' words carried the story in the first three of these elections. A news story might begin with a paragraph or two that set the tone, such as the size and mood of the crowd, but would then consist mainly of long quotes or paraphrases of the candidate's speech. However, in the most recent election they studied, 1984, the candidates' words appeared in short quotes and paraphrases.[31]

A parallel finding is the shrinking sound bite. In 1988 the average sound bite was less than ten seconds. Sound bites were slightly longer in 1992, but nowhere near the forty-two seconds they were in 1968.[32]

These findings reflect a trend toward an interpretive form of reporting that centers on the journalist's view of political reality, not the candidate's. The candidate's words are noteworthy largely insofar as they illustrate the journalist's chosen theme, which typically centers on the election's contestual aspects. The sound bite, or brief quote of the candidate's words, is seldom a thoughtful statement; it is nearly always an attack line. The predominance of clear-cut issues is a consequence.

This type of reporting makes the campaign look meaner, more chaotic, more manipulative, and more combative than it actually is. It highlights the disorganization of the campaign, and wrenches the candidates out of the context of their roles as leaders of electoral coalitions. In addition, it misrepresents the candidates' positions and priorities. Of all the issues they address, only those that can be fitted to the narrative line have much chance of making the news regularly.

This type of reporting, moreover, rests on a flimsy base. It is presented as a factual portrayal of the campaign, but it is laced with opinions. The press in all recent elections has expressed surprise that so many of its scenarios went wrong. "This year, the political world has changed so quickly, so many times, that even the pundits have grown wary of punditry," wrote the *New York Times*'s Robin Toner last summer.[33] Such statements are typically followed by broad generalizations about the inherent unpredictability of politics. However, the main reason the press's story lines often prove faulty is that they are based on an unreliable framework of analysis, which places too much emphasis on recent developments, marginal changes, and the actions of leaders, and too little emphasis on the steady currents of society.

Many of the recent changes in election journalism have improved it substantially. The change that placed the journalist in the role of speaking for the candidate is not, in my judgment, among them. It presumes that the press, rather than the political leader, should be charged with organizing public opinion. I would add that the presumption is uniquely American. The principle that governs election coverage in Britain, for example, is that "politics belongs to the politicians." The press's role is to "hold the ring," which means that its job is to facilitate political expression and debate. A comparative study of U.S. and British election coverage found that most news items in Britain originate with the politician, whereas in the United States they originate with the journalist. This study also found that quoted material from political leaders accounts for only 10 percent of television coverage of U.S. elections, as compared with 30 percent in the case of British elections.[34]

DIRECTIONS FOR REFORM: STRUCTURE

Changes in election journalism are not, by themselves, the route to a sound campaign. The problem remains that the press lacks the capacity to organize the campaign properly. To improve the flow of information in the campaign, the ability of political leaders and institutions to define the campaign must be improved.

The strength of the idea that the press can organize the campaign is evident in the extent to which reform proposals, and forums such as this one, concentrate on election journalism. Foundations and scholars could give more attention to studying the effect of political structures on communication and to educating political leaders about what they could do to make the campaign more coherent.

In this context, I offer two proposals:

1. Communication Structure: The Candidates' Imperative.
In a report that I wrote several years ago for the Alfred P. Sloan Foundation Commission on Presidential Selection, I argued that the presidential campaign should provide the candidates with adequate broadcast opportunities to present themselves and their policies as they wished to be seen. Candidates are responsible for their campaigns, and one of them will become president. It is imperative in the television age that they have significant opportunities to present their plans to the American people.

Before 1992, this imperative was not fully met. News coverage did not provide it, and although the televised conventions and debates provided significant opportunities, they were not themselves a sufficient forum. In my report to the Sloan Foundation Commission, I proposed a series of general-election broadcasts that included televised debates, speeches, and discussions. In 1991, the Joan Shorenstein Barone Center on the Press, Politics and Public Policy, at Harvard's John F. Kennedy School of Government, advanced a similar idea in its "Nine Sundays" proposal, which was written by John Ellis.

The "Nine Sundays" proposal recommended that the nine Sunday evenings between Labor Day and Election Day be devoted to candidate telecasts. There would be at least two debates between the presidential candidates and one vice-presidential debate. The final Sunday before Election Day would be devoted to back-to-back speeches by the candidates. The other Sunday evenings would be used for "conversations" with the candidates. Each conversation would be on a different issue, and the candidates, in back-to-back appearances, would be questioned by panelists. The telecasts, possibly excepting the debates and speeches, would be carried on a rotating basis by the major broadcast and cable networks.[35]

As it happened, the 1992 campaign fulfilled the candidates' imperative without the need for a television series of the "Nine Sundays" type. The four debates and the "new media" gave the candidates unprecedented opportunities to communicate directly with the voters. Moreover, the electorate's clear sense of what was important this election year helped to make the "new media" a forum for serious discussion. If candidates got a lot of soft questions on the call-in shows, they also got a fair number of tough ones.

There is no guarantee, however, that what happened in 1992 will become the norm. We know from past elections that the strategies and forms of televised campaigning can change rapidly. There was even a point in the 1992 campaign where the presidential debates appeared to be in jeopardy.

I believe it would be wise to institutionalize a series of general-election candidate telecasts that include debates and other candidate forums. This series would provide a fixed amount of time for the candidates to get their ideas across to the voters, and would give the voters regular access to the candidates over a substantial amount of time. This series would not preclude additional forums, such as the call-in shows and morning shows. However, the series, if it was on the scale of the "Nine Sundays" proposal, would include enough telecasts to give the candidates sufficient opportunities to speak directly with the American people.*

The basic principle for the series is that the telecasts would be designed to allow candidates to speak directly to the people, yet under conditions in which they could be held accountable for their remarks. Scrutiny must be a part of any television series that is intended to serve as a serious forum for bringing candidates and voters together. When the candidates' statements are subject to immediate scrutiny by journalists or others, the candidates are more likely to address the issues directly, and the electorate, in turn, is more likely to take an interest in what the candidates are saying.

---

* A similar broadcast series might be advisable during the campaign's nominating phase. Any set policy for this period, however, is confounded by questions of when the broadcasts should be held, who should participate, and whether they should be required of an incumbent president running for renomination. An ad hoc policy may be more advisable in the nominating phase.

The scrutiny feature will ensure that all of the telecasts, not just the debates, will feed into the news process. The telecasts will "make" news, because the candidates will be required to account for the positions they take, and for past behaviors that bear on these positions. In this way, the telecasts will help the press to present the campaign, and what the candidates represent, more fully and accurately.

The scrutiny feature is one reason I prefer a series of telecasts of the "Nine Sundays" variety to a free-time alternative. Most European political systems grant free broadcast time to parties and candidates, but I believe that a free-time policy makes less sense in our weak-party, presidential system than in a strong-party, parliamentary system. Moreover, free time may not serve the public interest as fully as is commonly assumed. In Britain, a few elections after the free-time policy had begun, 60 percent of the voters said they were dissatisfied with the programs, and a majority deliberately avoided exposure to them. The most common complaint was that the broadcasts were nothing but out-and-out attempts by the parties to sell their wares.[36]

I believe the idea of a series is also preferable to Paul Taylor's idea of a "five-minute fix." He suggests that during the final five weeks of the campaign each major candidate, on alternating nights, should receive five minutes of free time simultaneously on every broadcast station in the country. The only restriction would be that the candidate would have to appear on the air, alone, for the entire five minutes.[37] Compared with a televised series, the five-minute plan has several disadvantages: it would disrupt broadcasting, would provide the candidates with insufficient time to develop some of their arguments, and would take place without the immediate scrutiny of the candidates' statements.

Would Americans pay attention to a series of candidate telecasts? Critics who have insisted that the public is not interested in lengthy discussions of the issues were proved wrong by the huge audiences that tuned in to this year's debates and call-in shows. If these critics had paid close attention to the audiences for past debates, they would not have made the claim in the first place. Since 1960, there have been more than a dozen televised presidential debates during the general elections, and each had an audience well in excess of fifty million viewers. When presidential candidates appear together, and are subject to scrutiny, the American people are more than willing to listen and learn.

Three decades have passed since the first debates; the time has come to institutionalize them, and to present them in the context of a series of candidate-centered telecasts.

2. Campaign Structure: A Shorter and More Deliberative Process. For the most part, the problem of today's campaign lies deeper than the press. Disorganization is the hallmark of the presidential election system. The primaries are like wars waged between entrepreneurial candidates seeking to promote themselves, yet their support comes not from loyal armies but from groups and elites joined together solely for the election. There is no name associated with these factions, no continuing core of supporters, and typically the issues that dominate one campaign are unlike those emphasized in the previous campaign. These tenuous relationships put an extraordinary burden on voters, one that V. O. Key identified in his classic study of one-party politics in the South. "The voter is confronted," wrote Key, "with new faces, new choices, and must function in a sort of state of nature."[38]

It is this chaotic system that citizens and politicians alike expect the press to make intelligible. But the press, as we have seen, has neither the means nor the incentive to correct the system's weaknesses. What changes in the presidential campaign would diminish these weaknesses and hence increase the coherence of the news about it?

A provision to limit the campaign's length could improve campaign communication. The usual arguments against the lengthy campaign process are that it disrupts the policy process, bores the voters, and discourages responsible officeholders from seeking the presidency.

Long campaigns also foster a news agenda that exaggerates the influence of journalistic values. The fact is, there are not enough major issues for the candidates to keep their positions and priorities at the top of the news for an entire year. They can say all they have to say on the key issues in about two months; after that, all they can do is repeat their positions or take stands on lesser issues, neither of which is considered newsworthy. However, because a presidential campaign is considered inherently newsworthy, it gets covered even on those days when nothing terribly new or important happens. On such days in particular, reporters have greater freedom in their choice of news material. Not surprisingly, they are led to stories that reflect news values more than political ones.

The long campaign also appears to contribute to the bad-press tendency in election news. The campaign strains the relationship between the candidates and the press, such that the news gets nastier as the campaign goes along. My content analysis of the 1960–1988 campaigns indicates that there is, on average, a 30 percent increase in bad-news messages between the nominating and general-election stages.

A change that would have a great impact on the quality of the campaign, and on the quality of election news, would be to increase the party's importance in the nominating process. This paper is not the proper forum to discuss how the principle of party could be reasserted, whether through an extension of the superdelegate concept, a stacking of the primaries (which would increase the influence of the party elites), a preprimary convention to choose a party-endorsed candidate for nomination (which would increase their influence even more), or some other method.

Nevertheless, the positive consequences for election communication of a party-centered process should be noted. The party is the one intermediary capable of organizing electoral opinion in the nominating stage, which would give direction and coherence to the flow of information during the nominating process. Moreover, the campaign would be more firmly rooted in party traditions, which means that the maps that guide the voters in one election are like those they found reliable in past elections.

A foolproof electoral system is beyond reach. And it is easy to exaggerate the merits of a party-based system. But alternative ways of electing presidents are more or less prone to error. A workable system must take into account what the people, the parties, and the press can and cannot do. A sound electoral system is not based on the notion that the press can organize the voters' choices.

Notes

1. Walter Lippmann, *Public Opinion* (New York: Free Press, 1965), p. 19. Original publication date was 1922.

2. Ibid., p. 11.

3. Ibid., p. 226.

4. Carl Bernstein, "It's Press vs. Bush: A Bruising Fight," *Los Angeles Times*, October 25, 1992, p. M1.

5. Lippmann, *Public Opinion*, p. 226.

6. See *Mandate for Reform* (Washington, D.C.: Democratic National Committee, 1970).

7. This statement is based on an examination of the *New York Times* and the *Washington Post*.

8. Timothy Crouse, *The Boys on the Bus* (New York: Ballantine, 1973).

9. See, for example, Everett Carll Ladd, Jr., *American Political Parties* (New York: W. W. Norton, 1970), p. 2.

10. Michael Schudson, "What Time Means in a News Story," Occasional Paper no. 4, Gannett Center for Media Studies, Columbia University (New York, 1986), p. 3.

11. Carl Leubsdorf, "The Reporter and the Presidential Candidate," *Annals of the American Academy of Political and Social Science* 427 (September 1976): 6.

12. *Newsweek*, October 20, 1980, p. 65; George Will, "Debates Keep Them off the Streets," *Syracuse Post-Standard*, October 15, 1992, p. A10.

13. Michael Robinson and Margaret Sheehan, *Over the Wire and on TV* (New York: Russell Sage Foundation, 1983), p. 92–5.

14. Ibid., p. 99.

15. These data will be published in my forthcoming book, *Out of Order* (New York: Knopf).

16. See, for example, various issues of *Media Monitor*, 1992. Other confirmation comes from the 1992 study under the direction of Marion Ash, at the Barone Center, and from Matthew Kerbel's work at Villanova University.

17. Michael Robinson, "Improving Election Information in the Media" (Paper presented at Voting for Democracy Forum, Washington, D.C., September 1983), p. 2.

18. Gerald Pomper with Susan Lederman, *Elections in America* (New York: Dodd, Mead, 1976).

19. Michael G. Krukones, *Promises and Performance: Presidential Campaigns as Policy Predictors* (Lanham, Md.: University Press of America, 1984).

20. Ian Budge and Richard I. Hofferbert, "Mandates and Policy Outputs: U.S. Party Platforms and Federal Expenditures," *American Political Science Review* (March 1990): 111–32.

21. Pomper, *Elections in America*.

22. Colin Seymour-Ure, *The Political Impact of Mass Media* (Beverly Hills, Calif.: Sage, 1974), p. 223.

23. James David Barber, "Characters in the Campaign: The Literary Problem," in *Race for the Presidency*, ed. James David Barber (Englewood Cliffs, N.J.: Prentice Hall, 1978), pp. 114–15.

24. Example is from Jonathan Alter, "The Smear Heard 'Round the World," *Newsweek*, October 19, 1992, p. 27.

25. Thomas E. Patterson, *The Mass Media Election* (New York: Praeger, 1980), pp. 36–37.

26. Larry Sabato, *Feeding Frenzy: How Attack Journalism Has Transformed American Politics* (New York: Free Press, 1991), p. 1.

27. *Media Monitor*, October 1992, p. 5.

28. Benjamin I. Page, *Choices and Echoes in Presidential Elections* (Chicago: University of Chicago Press, 1978), ch. 6.

29. Patterson, *Mass Media Election*, pp. 34–35.

30. Lippmann, *Public Opinion*, p. 226.

31. Kristi Andersen and Stuart J. Thorson, "The Changing Meaning of Elections," (unpublished paper, Syracuse University, January 19, 1986).

32. Kiku Adatto, *The Shrinking Sound-Bite*, Joan Shorenstein Barone Center on the Press, Politics and Public Policy, John F. Kennedy School of Government, Harvard University, 1990, p. 5.

33. Robin Toner, "The Bounce: Blunt Reminders That It's Not Over until November 3," *New York Times,* July 19, 1992, p. E1.

34. Holly Semetko, Jay Blumler, Michael Gurevitch, and David Weaver, *The Formation of Campaign Agendas: A Comparative Analysis of Party and Media Roles in Recent American and British Elections* (Hillsdale, N.J.: Lawrence Erlbaum, 1991), pp. 60, 68, 74, 95, 98.

35. John Ellis, "Nine Sundays: A Proposal for Better Presidential Campaign Coverage," Joan Shorenstein Barone Center on the Press, Politics and Public Policy, John F. Kennedy School of Government, Harvard University, 1991.

36. Jay Blumler, Michael Gurevitch, and Julian Ives, "The Challenge of Election Broadcasting" (Unpublished paper, July 25, 1977), p. 10.

37. Paul Taylor, *See How They Run* (New York: Knopf, 1990), ch. 11.

38. V. O. Key, Jr., *Southern Politics* (New York: Vintage, 1949), p. 303.

INDEX

ABOUT THE AUTHORS

Kathleen Hall Jamieson is professor of communication and dean of the Annenberg School for Communication at the University of Pennsylvania. Her most recent book is *Dirty Politics: Deception, Distraction, and Democracy* (Oxford University Press, 1992). She is also the author of *Packaging the Presidency* (Oxford University Press, 1988) and *Eloquence in an Electronic Age* (Oxford University Press, 1988). She appeared weekly in the Public Affairs Television series "Listening to America" with Bill Moyers during the 1992 general election campaign.

Ken Auletta is the media columnist for the *New Yorker* and is the author of the bestseller, *Three Blind Mice: How the TV Networks Lost Their Way* (Random House, 1991). He writes a Sunday political column for the *New York Daily News*.

Thomas Patterson is professor of political science at the Maxwell School of Citizenship and Public Affairs at Syracuse University. He has written extensively on the subject of politics and elections, including three books, *The Unseeing Eye* (Putnam, 1976), *The Mass Media Election* (Praeger, 1980), and *The American Democracy* (McGraw-Hill, 1990). This article is based in his latest book, *Out of Order*, which will be published this fall by Knopf.